"This book is written for the experienced paddler, but is also useful for the novice, or for those wishing to decide which river to run with a commercial trip. Washington offers many exciting, challenging, and scenic whitewater runs, and this guidebook will introduce you to the best and most popular of them. If you plan to paddle whitewater in Washington, and want to know where to go and what to expect, you'll want a copy."

—CURRENTS Magazine

"A useful, ably written guidebook for intermediate-to-experienced rafters. Beginners can use it to select a river to have a pro take them down."

—THE WEEKLY

"The author is highly safety conscious and offers good information in a useful format: to each river segment he provides details for getting there plus the put-ins, take-outs, water levels, and other related information. It's very well done judging from my own experience."

—Verne Huser
RIVER RUNNER Magazine

"Those of us who guide rivers in Washington have been trading soggy napkin-maps of river areas for years. Finally there is a book on the subject—as a reference it's a terrific help. The river profiles are accurate, the maps nicely detailed and information sources indispensable."

—Dave Peevers
PACIFIC NORTHWEST Magazine

"The Evergreen State is uncommonly rich in good whitewater paddling. Pouring clean and cold from the snowcapped peaks of the Cascades and Olympics, Washington rivers offer 40 different runs within a three-hour drive of Seattle alone. How to select and describe some of the best? The author has defied the odds by producing an attractive text with a superb selection of rivers, straightforward descriptions and a broad range of information."

—Pam Miller
CANOE Magazine

WASHINGTON
SECOND 1 EDITION
WHITEWATER

by
Douglass A. North

The Mountaineers, Seattle

The Mountaineers: Organized 1906
". . . to explore and study the mountains, forests,
and watercourses of the Northwest."

Published by The Mountaineers
306 2nd Avenue West, Seattle, Washington 98119

Published simultaneously in Canada by Douglas & McIntyre
1615 Venables Street, Vancouver, B.C. V5L 2H1

Manufactured in the United States of America
Edited by Barbara Chasan
Designed by Bridget Culligan and Nick Gregoric
Cover photo: Popeye on the Middle Sauk
Title page photo: Exploring the Green River Gorge
Back cover photo: Confluence of North and South Forks of the Skykomish.

All photographs by Lorrie H. North unless otherwise credited.

Library of Congress Cataloging in Publication Data

North, Douglass A.
    Washington whitewater 1.

    Includes index.
    1. Rafting (Sports)—Washington (State)—Guide-books.
2. White-water canoeing—Washington (State)—Guide-books.
3. Washington (State)—Description and travel—
1981-   —Guide-books.   I. Title.   II. Title:
Washington whitewater one.   III. Title: Washington
white water 1.
GV776.W2N67   1988   917.97   87-34898
ISBN 0-89886-158-6 (pbk.)

Whitewater and Green Mountain on the Upper Middle Fork Snoqualmie

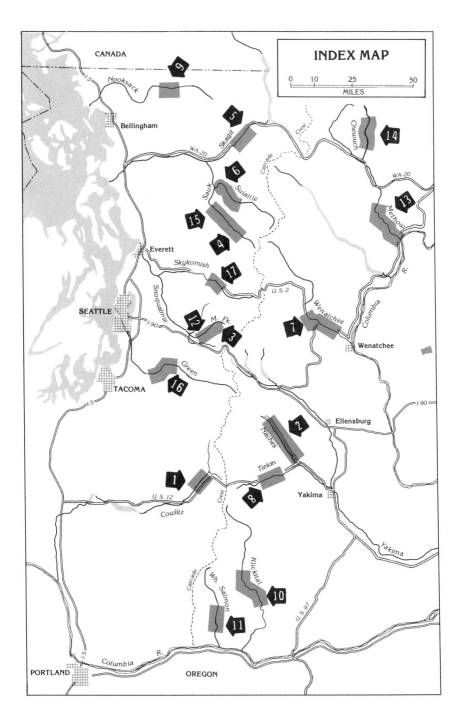

INDEX MAP

0   10   25   50
MILES

CANADA

Nooksack

Bellingham

WA-20

Skagit

Crest

Cascade

Chewuch

Sauk

Suiattle

Methow

Everett

Skykomish

U.S. 2

Snoqualmie

Wenatchee

Columbia R.

SEATTLE

I-90

M. Fk.

Wenatchee

Green

I-5

TACOMA

I-90

Ellensburg

Naches

Tieton

Cowlitz

U.S. 12

Crest

Yakima

Yakima

Cascade

Wh. Salmon

Klickitat

U.S. 97

Columbia R.

PORTLAND

I-5

OREGON

Contents

Preface

River guidebooks take two basic approaches. One paints a general picture of the river, provides the essential information on put-ins, take-outs and river difficulty, and leaves the reader to explore the river himself. The other approach provides the reader with all of the verifiable information possible on the river, including descriptions and locations of rapids, landmarks and possible campsites. Each approach has advantages and disadvantages; some people may prefer one to the other.

The principal advantage of the less detailed guidebook is that it forces the boater to rely on his own resources. Its advocates point out that river channels constantly change, so recording the location of all rapids and landmarks as if they were static could be misleading.

The detailed river logs in this book obviously place it in the second category. These logs have several advantages:

1. They allow the boater who has never run the river to figure out where he is.

2. They allow boaters to choose put-ins and take-outs for the part of the river they wish to run.

3. They provide a graphical representation of the difficulty and intensity of each part of the trip.

4. They allow government agencies to precisely locate the important rapids and the most scenic sections for river conservation purposes.

5. They keep the author honest. Providing a detailed river log is impossible without having actually run the river, usually several times. Some authors are willing to include in their guidebooks rivers they have heard about but have never run. Their "information" is often woefully inaccurate.

The first *Washington Whitewater,* published four years ago, has been well received. This revision updates the information on put-ins and take-outs (and man-made changes such as the Wenatchee dam), provides more background information and adds two new chapters, one on the Upper Middle Fork of the Snoqualmie and one on the Chewuch. It also gives more conservation information about the rivers.

An important reason for writing a guidebook is to promote river conservation. *Washington Whitewater* and *Washington Whitewater 2* have introduced many boaters to the beauty and excitement of the rivers of this state. They have helped build a constituency of boaters to protect these rivers. A politically vigorous group of Washington boaters is vital to saving our free-flowing rivers. Over 100 dam license applications are pending for hydroelectric projects on Washington rivers. In a few years, the bottom 1.7 miles of the Cispus River (in *Washington Whitewater 2*) will disappear beneath the slack waters behind the Cowlitz Falls project. A battle now rages to save the North Fork of the Snoqualmie (also in *Washington Whitewater 2*) from inundation by a

Horseshoe Bend *on the Naches*

water supply project. There have been dams proposed on many of the rivers in this book, including the Cowlitz, Skagit, Middle Fork Snoqualmie and Skykomish. To save these rivers, boaters must actively oppose these projects.

Washington Whitewater 1 and *2* are designed to promote continued river conservation work. They will introduce you to many new rivers and, hopefully, get you involved in their protection. Concerned whitewater boaters in the Northwest have formed the Northwest Rivers Council, with chapters in Washington, Oregon, Idaho and Montana. We cover the same geographic region as the Northwest Power Planning Council. The Northwest Rivers Council has taken an active role in the Northwest Rivers Study conducted by the Power Planning Council to determine future dam sites in the Northwest. We have intervened as a party in Federal Energy Regulatory Commission dam licensing proceedings, participated in the planning process with the National Forests and, along with the Washington Wilderness Coalition, begun work on a Wild & Scenic Rivers bill for Washington.

If you enjoy Washington's rivers, get involved! Contact:

Northwest Rivers Council
P.O. Box 88
Seattle, WA 98111
(206) 547-7886

Acknowledgments

This book is dedicated to the hard-working volunteers and staff of the Northwest Rivers Council who keep these rivers flowing free for all of us to enjoy.

I would like to express my love and appreciation to my wife Lorrie. Without her tolerance of my mania for rivers, these books would not be possible.

I also gratefully acknowledge the assistance and kind permission of John Garren to use the river log system that he developed in *Oregon River Tours* and *Idaho River Tours*. He developed much of the river data in the introduction to explain the background and use of the river log system.

Finally, thanks go to Professor Joel M. Andress and geography students Shane Straga, George Stuart, Julie Lacefield and Judy Houston at Central Washington University, who drew the maps for this book.

Introduction

This guidebook is for intermediate, advanced and expert rafters or kayakers who already know the basics of controlling their boats in rapids. It is *not* for beginners to use by themselves. If you do not already know how to handle a raft or kayak in class 2 water, you are not yet ready to undertake the trips in this book without expert help. The' beginning boater should look first to books on technique and equipment, such as the *Whitewater River Book* by Ron Watters.

Because it is essential to know the water level of a river in order to run it safely, I selected rivers for which representative gauge readings are available. To increase the likelihood of a pleasant experience for everyone, I chose rivers that normally have sufficient water to allow you to run them in a raft for at least three weeks from April through September.

Although some smaller rivers have enough water to be boated nearly every year, their frequent logjams make boating difficult. I have excluded rivers with insufficient flow to move the logs to one side of the river. This does not mean that you will never encounter a log all the way across these rivers, but it is unusual. However, you should always remain alert.

Washington Whitewater 1 and *Washington Whitewater 2* describe nearly all the rivers in this state which (1) have significant whitewater, (2) allow rafting, as well as kayaking during the warm months of the year, (3) have fairly reliable water level information available on them and (4) do not suffer from chronic logjams.

River Classification

There are formal, recognized methods of classifying rivers according to difficulty. This is of particular advantage to the beginning boater so that he may select rivers, or sections of rivers, within his capability. The following is a summary of the International River Classification System:

Class 1. Easy and Novice

Sand banks, bends without difficulty, occasional small rapids with waves regular and low. Correct course easy to find. River velocity less than hard backpaddling speed from 0-4 miles per hour. Spray cover or decking for canoes unnecessary. River drop approximately 0-5 feet per mile.

Class 2. Medium or Intermediate

Fairly frequent but unobstructed rapids, regular waves, easy eddies and river bends. Course easy to recognize. River velocity occasionally exceeding hard backpaddling, velocity from 2-6 miles per hour. Spray covers for canoe useful. River drop 5-15 feet per mile.

Class 3. Difficult or Expert

Maneuvering in rapids necessary. Powerful eddies, standing waves, course difficult to read, scouting may be required, lining should be considered. Canoes require spray covers. River drop 10-25 feet per mile. River velocity 4-8 miles per hour.

Class 4. Very Difficult or Expert

Difficult broken water, long extended rapids, standing waves and eddies, powerful hydraulics, course difficulty requires scouting, lining may be necessary. River drop exceeds 30 feet per mile. River velocities over 6 miles per hour.

Class 5. Exceedingly Difficult

Extremely complicated rapids with powerful hydraulics. River conditions are only attempted by the very experienced.

Class 6. Dangerous

River running involves substantial hazard to life.

It is almost impossible to rate a whole river under this system, but the classification is useful in describing a particular rapid. Generally, any major rapid is class 3 or more and should be approached with some caution. Ratings in this book are conservative. Thus, if there is a question between two rating classes, the higher rating is used.

You should keep in mind that each rapid differs slightly at every water level. However, the same rapids present the most serious challenges on a given stretch regardless of the water level. Ultimately, it is your responsibility to match your ability to the river you intend to run.

In order to provide some help to you in evaluating the difficulty of the rivers in this book, the trips are described from *least* to *most* difficult — from the Cowlitz to the Skykomish. The runs are grouped into three sections: intermediate, advanced and expert. An intermediate boater knows the rules of whitewater safety, understands hypothermia and basic river hydraulics, and can control his boat in moderate rapids — class 2 with some easy class 3. The intermediate runs either have rapids no more difficult than class 2 or the major rapids can be easily inspected from the road before putting in, allowing you to decide whether you are capable of running them before you start.

Know your whitewater abilities! (Kevin O'Brien photo)

An advanced boater thoroughly understands river hydraulics, runs class 3 rapids with confidence and has good river reading skills. All of the advanced runs have either demanding class 3 rapids that cannot be easily seen from the road or they have nearly continuous class 2 and 3 rapids that require substantial experience to run safely.

An expert boater has excellent river reading skills, runs class 3 rapids without scouting and remains confident in class 4 water. The expert runs involve class 4 rapids and, often, nearly continuous class 3.

Boaters in open canoes should approach these rivers with great caution. The intermediate rivers can be canoed by very good canoeists, after careful scouting. All the advanced rivers have class 3 rapids which will swamp an open canoe. Only expert whitewater canoeists running the river at low water are likely to make it down these rivers with both themselves and their canoes intact. The expert rivers verge on being impossible to canoe even for expert whitewater canoeists.

Decked canoes are capable of running any water that a kayak can, and all references to kayaks in this book include decked canoes as well.

Washington Rivers

Boaters from other states who are not familiar with continuous rapids should approach Washington rivers with caution. In many other parts of the country, the rivers are pool and drop with substantial stretches of calm water between the rapids. Very few Washington rivers are pool and drop. Most have continuous fast water that offers little opportunity to recover from an upset before the next rapid. Some of the rivers have such continuous rapids that eddies are rare enough to be landmarks.

Washington rivers have continuous fast water because their river valleys are fairly broad and smoothly sloped. The valleys were formed by glaciers in the last ice age and have the U shape characteristic of glacial valleys. Washington had particularly heavy glaciers in the last ice age due to its northern location and its heavy precipitation.

Because the glaciers carved broad valleys with even gradients, Washington's highway engineers have built roads along nearly all of the major river valleys in the state. (Due to dense vegetation, however, the roads are not usually visible from the rivers.) This is in contrast with other states (such as California, Oregon and Idaho) that have large river valleys with no roads in them. Often the river valleys in these states are narrow defiles cut solely by the river's erosion. Thus, highway engineers have frequently avoided the river valleys in favor of the plateaus between.

Selecting a River

Know your abilities and select a river suitable for your skill level. Generally at least one intermediate, advanced or expert run is at a runnable water level at all times from April through July. The Runnable Seasons table (following) will help you pick a river that is likely to be at a good water level.

RUNNABLE SEASONS

Trip	Recommended Water Level (in cubic feet per second) and gauge location.	Month											
		J	F	M	A	M	J	J	A	S	O	N	D
1 Cowlitz	1,400 - 3,200 Packwood						●						
2 Naches	1,200 - 2,600 Cliffdell					●	●						
3 Upper Middle Fork Snoqualmie	1,200 - 3,500 Middle Fork	●					●				●	●	
4 Upper Sauk	5,500 - 12,000 Sauk						●	●					
5 Skagit	1,500 - 5,500 Newhalem	●	●	●	●	●	●		●	●	●	●	●
6 Suiattle	2,500 - 9,000 Sauk	●	●	●	●	●	●			●	●	●	●
7 Wenatchee	4,000 - 15,000 Peshastin					●	●						
8 Tieton	1,000 - 2,200 Rimrock								●				
9 North Fork Nooksack	600 - 1,600 North Fork						●	●	●	●			
10 Klickitat	1,700 - 3,500 Pitt					●	●						
11 White Salmon	700 - 1,300 Underwood						●	●			●		
12 Middle Middle Fork Snoqualmie	1,500 - 3,000 Middle Fork	●									●	●	
13 Methow	3,000 - 11,000 Pateros					●	●						
14 Chewuch	5,000 - 10,000 Pateros					●	●						
15 Middle Sauk	4,000 - 10,000 Sauk					●	●	●					
16 Green	1,100 - 2,300 Howard Hansen	●	●	●							●	●	●
17 Skykomish	2,000 - 5,000 Goldbar	●	●	●			●			●	●	●	●

Water Level

Water level is one of the most important factors a boater should consider. There is a relatively narrow range of water levels for any river that makes for a good trip. Below some minimum level, the stream velocity decreases, the rocks (stream roughness) become more troublesome and the trip more difficult. Conversely, above a certain level, the stream velocity becomes so high and the river hydraulics so powerful as to make safe boating impossible. This is particularly true on rivers with very high average slopes like many of those in this book.

Fortunately, government agencies maintain a large system of stream gauges on almost all major rivers. The gauge heights are translated into cubic feet per second, abbreviated as cfs, a measure of the volume of water passing by the gauge in one second. Each whitewater trip in

Beware of the power of high water

this book is referenced to a specific water level on the particular trip, along with recommended water levels. I have tried to use representative gauges wherever possible. Sometimes it has been necessary, however, to use a gauge on another part of the river, because it is the only one from which up-to-date readings can be obtained.

Kayakers can usually run a river at a lower water level than rafters; thus, many of the descriptions mention a lower minimum water level suitable for kayakers. The recommended level is the one for rafts because kayakers will also generally find the higher water level more enjoyable, with better holes to play in.

You can check on the current water level by calling the tape-recorded message prepared by the National Oceanic and Atmospheric Administration (NOAA) at (206) 526-8530. The tape is updated every Monday, Wednesday and Friday morning from April through November. From December through March, the tape provides Steelheader's Hotline information on river levels. If you can't get the information you need from the tape, call NOAA at (206) 526-6087. For some rivers I have listed another agency that can provide gauge information as well. The tape should be your main source of information because the other agencies are primarily concerned with flood control and warnings and do not welcome calls from river runners. Call them only if you cannot get the information you need from the tape.

The Runnable Seasons table shows you the time of year when the average flow of the river is within the recommended water level. Of course, the river frequently varies from the average flow, so check the water level. Since most people like to boat in the warm months of the year, the times listed as best at the beginning of each chapter are only the warmer months.

Slope

River slope is usually measured by boaters in feet of river drop per mile. It can be scaled from conventional U. S. Geological Survey contour maps. Steep slopes have high river velocity and will usually, but not necessarily, have difficult rapids. The slope listed at the beginning of each chapter is the average for the trip.

Most of the trips in this book have high average slopes. Many famous whitewater trips in other states have more gentle slopes. The Colorado in the Grand Canyon has a slope of 8 feet per mile, the Salmon River in Idaho 12 feet per mile. In this book, the Skagit has a slope in this range, but the rest of the trips have much higher slopes, ranging up to the North Fork of the Nooksack at 53 feet per mile. High slopes make for faster trips and more constant whitewater.

Roughness

River roughness greatly influences river difficulty. The rocky, "rough" stream channel provides the basis for a wide variety of stream hydraulics that form rapids.

A relatively uniform stream slope and smooth channel (such as the Cowlitz) usually provide easy river boating. Rough channels with steeper river slopes often end up with names like Boulder Drop, Black Canyon Rapids, Mercury and Jaws.

RELATIVE USE

	River	Commercial Use	General Use
1	Cowlitz	None	Light
2	Naches	Light	Light
3	Upper Middle Fork Snoqualmie	None	Light
4	Upper Sauk	Light	Moderate
5	Skagit	Moderate	Moderate
6	Suiattle	Heavy	Heavy
7	Wenatchee	Extreme	Extreme
8	Tieton	Extreme*	Extreme*
9	North Fork Nooksack	Light	Light
10	Klickitat	Light	Moderate
11	White Salmon	Moderate	Heavy
12	Middle Middle Fork Snoqualmie	Light	Moderate
13	Methow	Heavy	Heavy
14	Chewuch	None	Light
15	Middle Sauk	Moderate	Moderate
16	Green	Light	Moderate
17	Skykomish	Heavy	Heavy

*Tieton use is extreme only in September. It is light in June when the river often reaches runnable levels.

Difficulty

The factors of water level, slope and roughness are the major criteria to consider in evaluating river difficulty. All of these factors play a role in the formation of rapids, and rapids are the principal determinant for river difficulty. Several other factors are more subjective, such as ease of rescue, water temperature or remoteness of the river. Indirectly, all of these factors are considered when evaluating the rapids' classifications.

Once you have found a river of suitable difficulty and water level, look at that chapter and see whether the scenery, camping and rapids descriptions suit your needs. If you seek solitude, consult the Relative Use table.

Length of Runs

Some of the runs are much longer than others and lend themselves to overnight trips if you would like to do some river camping. The Methow and Klickitat would make good overnight trips, as would both the Upper and Middle Sauk or the Upper and Middle Snoqualmie, run as one trip. The following table lists the length of each trip.

A rough channel contributes to the difficulty of the Green River Gorge

The Upper Naches

WHITEWATER RUNS*

Rating		River	Length of Run in miles
Intermediate Rivers	**1**	Cowlitz	8
	2	Naches	26
	3	Upper Middle Fork Snoqualmie	7
	4	Upper Sauk	8
	5	Skagit	9
Advanced Rivers	**6**	Suiattle	13
	7	Wenatchee	19
	8	Tieton	12
	9	North Fork Nooksack	8
	10	Klickitat	18
	11	White Salmon	7
	12	Middle Middle Fork Snoqualmie	8
	13	Methow	26
Expert Rivers	**14**	Chewuch	13
	15	Middle Sauk	10
	16	Green	14
	17	Skykomish	7

*This ranking is based on the difficulty of controlling your boat. Estimating the danger to swimmers in the event of upset would be different. As an example, the Suiattle's logjams present a great danger of death to swimmers who may be swept into them. Thus, it requires less skill to boat the Suiattle than the Wenatchee, but there is greater danger in boating the Suiattle.

Using the River Map and Log

The river map and log contain most of the information you need on the river. Both the log and map use the standard river convention of placing upstream at the bottom of the page and downstream at the top so that the log and map show the river flowing away from you. The maps and logs correlate so that you can see where you are on both simultaneously by referring to river miles. River miles are counted from the mouth so that they go down in number as you go down the river.

The river log depicts features that can actually be seen by a boater on the river. Thus, some of the maps show features that are useful reference points but do not appear on the logs and some of the text refers to features that are not on the logs because these features can't be seen from the river. The maps often show a larger area than

The log shows you what you can see from the river

It's particularly important to watch for changes in the channel on small rivers

indicated on the logs so that the user can get oriented more easily for making shuttles.

The log and map can be taped on the cowling of a kayak or the frame of a raft. Only a few symbols are necessary to describe most of the things a boater can identify on the river. Of course, it isn't possible to follow the log while running a river with continuous difficult rapids such as the Gorge section of the Green River or the Upper Sauk. On these rivers, you consult the log whenever you stop, and check on the landmarks which you need to remember for the next portion of the trip.

Remember that the river logs are not engraved in stone. River channels can change overnight with flood, landslide, earthquake or even a big tree falling across the river. If you see anything peculiar, such as freshly toppled trees that still have green leaves on them piling up around a bend, get out and scout from shore!

The river logs are measured in units of time rather than distance. This is because the speed with which a boater progresses downriver changes frequently as the slope of the riverbed changes. Time remains constant, however, and you can easily gain a sense of how long it will take to get to the next rapid in comparison with how long it took you to get to the last one. I don't expect that you will actually use a watch to time your progress downriver, but only that the log will give you a feel for how long it will take you to get to the next point of interest.

In planning your trip, you should expect that the total time on the river, including stops, will be about one and one-half to two times the amount of time shown on the log.

Symbols for the Logs

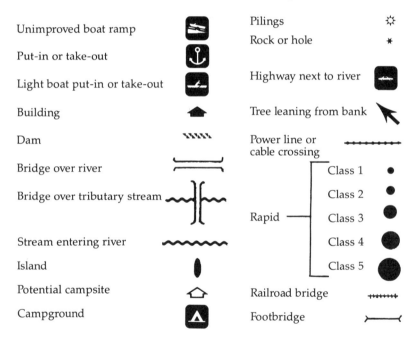

Unimproved boat ramp

Put-in or take-out

Light boat put-in or take-out

Building

Dam

Bridge over river

Bridge over tributary stream

Stream entering river

Island

Potential campsite

Campground

Pilings

Rock or hole

Highway next to river

Tree leaning from bank

Power line or cable crossing

Rapid — Class 1
Class 2
Class 3
Class 4
Class 5

Railroad bridge

Footbridge

Relative Drift Time

The relative drift time for various boats differs significantly. Log times in this book are for a 10-man raft at a particular river stage. (If you wonder why a raft was always used, try keeping track of time while taking detailed notes and paddling a kayak.) For the same type boat and approximate river stage there is little difference in time.

Kayaks, however, move downriver about one and one-half times faster than a raft (unless they are playing in a hole, of course); consequently, kayakers should find that it takes them only about two-thirds the time shown in the log to cover any portion of the run.

Safety

Anyone using this book on a river should already be very familiar with whitewater safety. Just as a reminder, however, the following points should be borne in mind:

1. Wear a lifejacket at all times. The biggest cause of death on a river, bar none, is the failure to wear a lifejacket. Everyone should wear a Coast Guard approved type I, III, or V lifejacket.

2. Never boat a river beyond your ability. You should always be capable of running the hardest rapid on the stretch of river that you intend to run. Know the River Classification System and your ability.

Make sure you have all the proper safety equipment you need

The cold water of Washington rivers always presents a danger of hypothermia. (NW Outdoor Center photo)

3. Never boat a river at too high a water level. This is probably the next biggest killer after failure to wear a lifejacket. Consequently, this book recommends a range of water levels for each river and tells you where to call to find out the gauge readings.

4. Always be aware of the threat of hypothermia. It is nearly always necessary to wear a wetsuit when running the rivers of western Washington. Most of the water in these rivers is recently melted ice and snow. Hypothermia strikes in three to five minutes. Wetsuits are often necessary in eastern Washington, too, and wool clothing should always be kept handy.

5. Always boat with an organized group. There should be at least two boats in your party if both are large rafts (larger than six-man) and at least three boats if any are not large rafts. Everyone in the group should be trained in how to rescue boaters in the event of upset.

6. Be aware of the danger presented by sweepers and strainers. Sweepers and strainers are downed logs and brush in the river. They present a much greater danger of death to swimmers than do rocks because the water flowing through them can easily pin a swimmer under water. Boaters must be careful to stay away from brush and logjams.

7. Be aware of the danger presented by dams and weirs. These man-made river obstructions create perfect hydraulics which can prove deadly with only a 2-foot drop. They are the second most dangerous obstacles on a river after sweepers and strainers.

8. Wear a helmet at all times when you kayak and in class 4 or 5 water when you raft. The rocky channels generally present in class 4 or 5 rapids pose a considerable danger to the head of anyone thrown out of a boat. Kayakers should wear helmets at all times because of the ease with which they may suddenly find themselves upside-down.

Because of the difficulty of these runs, kayakers should be familiar with the Eskimo Roll, and all boaters should be prepared to remove a boat pinned on rocks.

Whitewater rafting and kayaking entails unavoidable risks that every river runner assumes, realizes and respects. This guide assumes that you understand those risks. The fact that a section of river is described in this book and is rated for difficulty does not mean that it necessarily will be safe for you. Rivers vary greatly in difficulty and in the amount and kind of preparation needed to enjoy them safely. And because rivers are dynamic systems, conditions frequently change with the weather, seasons and other factors.

You minimize the risks by being knowledgeable, prepared and alert. There is not space in this book for a general treatise on white-water rafting or kayaking, but a number of good books and courses teach these skills. It is essential that you be aware both of your own limitations and of existing conditions at the time and place of your outing. If river conditions require greater skill or experience than you possess, or if factors such as weather or the condition of your craft, yourself or your companions are such as to dangerously increase the risk of running a river, change your plans. It is better to have wasted a day or two than to invite serious injury or fatality.

These warnings are not intended to warn qualified whitewater boaters off the rivers described in this guide. Many people enjoy safe kayaking or rafting trips down these rivers every year. However, one element of the beauty, freedom and excitement of river running is the presence of risks that do not confront us at home. When you kayak or raft down a whitewater river, you take on those risks. You can meet them safely, but only if you exercise your own independent judgment and common sense.

River Ethics

Part of river conservation is making sure that your enjoyment does not degrade the river's natural qualities or harm its fish and wildlife. If our children and grandchildren are to enjoy our rivers and the wild creatures that visit them, we must take care to leave the river environment no worse than we find it. To ensure the enjoyment of our rivers for everyone, keep the following rules in mind.

1. Respect private property. Don't put in, take out or stop on private property without the owner's permission. Certainly, don't take anything, such as fruit or wood. Nothing will restrict our use of rivers faster than alienating local landowners.

2. Don't leave anything behind. This applies to litter, equipment and even evidence of fire. Pack it *all* out.

3. Use a stove or firepan. Use of fire is not common on Washington rivers because nearly all rivers can be run in one day, but if you have a fire, put it in a firepan. A firepan prevents charring the ground and killing the micro-organisms in the soil. It also makes packing the ashes out with you easy; and no one can tell that you had a fire. Always have a shovel along (in addition to your bailing bucket) anytime you have a fire.

4. Dispose of human waste and waste water above the high water mark. It will decompose faster if buried in the top 6-8 inches of soil. Pack out all toilet paper in a plastic sack. Use biodegradable soap.

The Skykomish should be added to the federal Wild & Scenic Rivers System. (Doug North photo)

5. Respect the privacy of others. Don't stop to eat or camp where others have stopped; find your own site downriver. Keep quiet while passing other groups on the river; they may be appreciating nature's tranquility.

6. Don't disturb wildlife. Many animals and birds nest and feed along rivers and can be seriously disturbed by boaters coming unnecessarily close, perhaps to take a picture.

River shorelines are a particularly fragile and much used environment. Treat them with respect so that we can continue to enjoy them in the future.

River Protection Programs

There are two major programs available to protect Washington's rivers from dams and development and to preserve them for fish, wildlife, recreation and scenery.

Federal Wild & Scenic Rivers Act

Under the Wild & Scenic Rivers Act, a segment of a river is eligible to become part of the Wild & Scenic Rivers system if it is free-flowing and has one or more outstandingly remarkable values (such as scenery, fish and wildlife, recreation, geology, history, culture or ecology). To become "Wild & Scenic" the river most often has to be designated by an act of Congress. Congress usually requires that a study of the river be done before it is added to the system. The study can either be done at the direction of Congress or by a federal land-managing agency (such as the Forest Service) as part of its planning process.

Federal Wild & Scenic river segments are classified according to how much development they have along them. *Wild* river segments can be accessible only by water or by trail and have very few human-made structures along them. Although there are some Washington river segments that qualify as wild, none have yet been designated. *Scenic* river segments can be paralleled by roads as long as the roads are generally not visible and there are very few bridges or buildings along them. In Washington, the Sauk, Suiattle, Cascade and White Salmon have the only Scenic River segments designated under the Act. *Recreational* river segments can have a great deal of development along them if, at the same time, they have outstanding natural river values. The Skagit and lower Klickitat (near the Columbia Gorge) are designated as Recreational river segments.

The Green River Gorge would make an excellent addition to our state Scenic Rivers Program

Federal Wild & Scenic designation protects a river from all dams and water projects and limits further development along its banks. State and local governments control development. The general idea is that homes, farms and cabins already there can stay, but new building should be back from the bank, where it can't be seen from the river. The act prohibits the use of condemnation to acquire land if over half the land along the river is already owned by the government; this is true for all the rivers proposed for Wild & Scenic designation in Washington. After designation, a management plan is drawn up for the river in order to protect its scenery, fish, wildlife and recreation.

Washington State Scenic Rivers Program

The state Scenic Rivers Program protects scenic rivers of special value to the citizens of Washington State. Rivers must be added to the program by an act of the state legislature. There is a Committee of Participating Agencies, which oversees the program and is charged with making recommendations to the legislature on new rivers to be added. The program is administered through the state Parks and Recreation Commission. The commission is currently engaged in studying Washington's rivers to determine which ones should be recommended to the legislature.

The state Scenic Rivers Program directly affects only state, city and county land. It does not affect private land, but it does direct local governments (which administer the zoning and shorelines management programs) to act in a manner consistent with the Scenic Rivers Program. Federal agencies that license or build dams are required to consider whether or not a river is in this program, but they can decide to build a dam even though the river is in the state program.

After a river is added to the state Scenic Rivers Program, a management plan for the river is to be drawn up. State Parks and Recreation is in the process of drawing up a management plan for the one river that is in the system: the Skykomish (along with the North Fork Sky, South Fork, Beckler and Tye).

The state program is definitely weaker than the federal Wild & Scenic Rivers Act, but it is a good choice for those rivers (such as the Green, lower Methow and lower Wenatchee) where there is no federal land and where federal protection is therefore unlikely. State designation makes money available to acquire river access, camping and picnicking sites, which can lessen conflicts with local landowners.

The state Scenic Rivers Program deserves our support. If you would like to help protect rivers under it, contact the Northwest Rivers Council (listed in the Preface) or:

Steve Starlund
Washington State Scenic Rivers Program
Washington State Parks and Recreation Commission
7150 Cleanwater Lane
Olympia, WA 98504

Department of Wildlife
Conservation Licenses

The Washington State Department of Wildlife (which was called the Department of Game before July 1987) requires everyone using its river access sites to have a license. You can have either a fishing license or a conservation license. A conservation license is issued for a calendar year and in 1987 cost $8. You can use it an unlimited number of times within the year. It entitles you, your spouse and any children under 18 accompanying you to park at and use the department's river access points (mentioned in this book on the Wenatchee, Methow, Klickitat and Skykomish). Anyone using a department access site without a license will be ticketed by a department officer.

1

Cowlitz

Logged at -	1,500 cfs Packwood gauge
Recommended water level -	1,400 to 3,200 cfs
Best time -	Late June to late July
Rating -	Intermediate
Water level information -	NOAA Tape (206) 526-8530
	NOAA Information (206) 526-6087
River mile -	134.8 to 126.5; 8.3 miles
Time -	2 hours, 9 minutes; 3.9 mph
Elevation -	1255' to 1050'; 25' per mile

La Wis Wis to Packwood

The first mile and a half of this trip are very beautiful. You will pass between towering rock walls and under the branches of virgin evergreens that overhang the channel. The crystalline water collects in deep green pools, then flows into straight-forward, fun rapids. Enjoy this portion of the trip — once the Muddy Fork of the Cowlitz joins the channel, the scenery is much less spectacular.

The name Cowlitz comes from an Indian name which had many different spellings but was applied both to the river and to the Salish tribe which lived along its banks. Its exact meaning has been lost, but it is roughly translated as "capturing the medicine spirit" since the tribe used a prairie along the river for young braves to commune with the Great Spirit.

Getting There

The Cowlitz runs along US 12, 67 miles east of I-5. To reach it from western Washington north of Tacoma, take State Routes 410 and 123, which cross Cayuse Pass east of Mt. Rainier. If you are planning a trip between November and April, check before you set out to be sure the pass is not closed by snow.

There are beautiful cliffs along the upper Cowlitz

Put-ins and Take-outs

To reach two of the three popular put-ins, you will have to enter La Wis Wis Campground, clearly marked on US 12. Note that the campground is only open from Memorial Day weekend through mid-November. If you would like to get into the area at any other time, call the Packwood Ranger Station, (206) 494-5515.

Small groups with lightweight boats may want to use the uppermost put-in. To reach it, take the first right after entering the campground. The put-in is a narrow and fairly steep 15-foot path to the river, near the bridge over the Clear Fork of the Cowlitz. You can't park here, and you will have to unload the boats quickly, then drive to parking elsewhere.

Large parties and groups needing to inflate rafts will want to drive straight ahead on the road into the campground. Beyond some campsites is the put-in, just below the confluence of the Clear Fork of the Cowlitz and the Ohanapecosh rivers.

You can also put in or take out at Jody's Bridge, about a mile from US 12 on Forest Service 1270 road. The road turns off US 12 about two miles south of La Wis Wis Campground and 4.5 miles north of Packwood. Coming from the north, the road leaves US 12 just beyond a yellow highway sign indicating a road leaving the opposite side of the highway from 1270 and going to Lava Creek.

To reach the take-out, turn off US 12 in the middle of Packwood onto the Skate Creek Road. The take-out is on the left bank, just downstream from the bridge over the river.

Water Level

The Cowlitz is a good run at 1400 to 3200 cfs on the Packwood gauge. Canoeists and kayakers may be able to run it down to about 1200 cfs if they don't mind hitting a few rocks.

Cowlitz
Packwood Gauge
Recommend 1,400 to 3,200 cfs

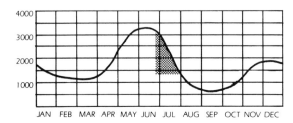

Special Hazards

None.

Scenery

The first mile and a half to two miles of the trip are breath-taking. Many kayakers and canoeists may want to run the upper section to Jody's Bridge, then take out and go back up to run the section again. The scenery deteriorates as soon as the Muddy Fork of the Cowlitz River joins the channel. It's interesting to watch the water of the

Clear Fork mix with the silt-laden Muddy Fork, but within 200 yards, the whole river is gray. The channel becomes braided and winds constantly around many islands and gravel bars. However, from the wider river channel, you will have good views of Mt. Rainier and the surrounding mountains.

Camping

Because La Wis Wis Campground is large, you will probably be able to find sites there except on holiday weekends. It is a beautiful campground — a fee is charged.

If you are with a large group or want a more private site, ask at the Packwood Ranger Station, (206) 494-5515. Sites are available near Jody's Bridge and up State Route 123, along the Ohanapecosh near Mt. Rainier National Park. But don't camp on the land along the river below log time 45 minutes; it is generally privately owned.

Rapids

The rapids on this trip are straight-forward, and you won't need to scout them except at water levels higher than those recommended. You will encounter the most difficult maneuvering at the two head-walls at log time 15 minutes. You will have to be positioned in advance to pull off first the right bank and then the left bank. The rapid at log time 1:50 provides the largest waves of the trip in a drop that funnels all the river's water through a gap about 35 feet wide.

The banks of the upper part are heavily forested

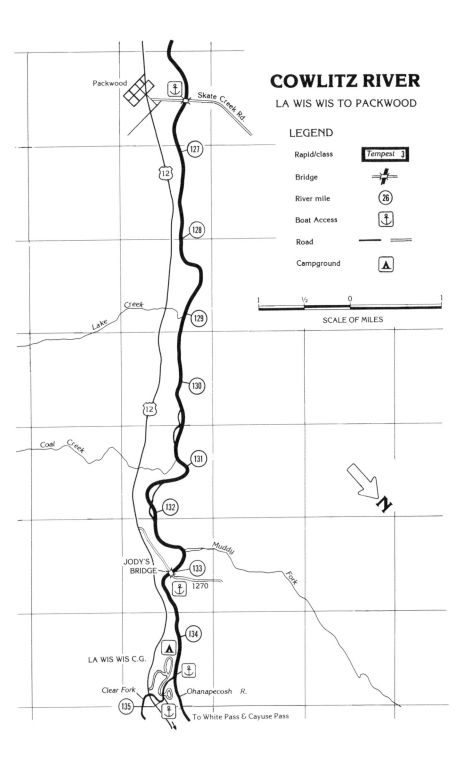

COWLITZ RIVER

LA WIS WIS TO PACKWOOD

LEGEND

Rapid/class	Tempest 3
Bridge	
River mile	26
Boat Access	
Road	
Campground	

1   ½   0   1

SCALE OF MILES

Packwood

Skate Creek Rd.

127

12

128

Lake Creek

129

130

12

Coal Creek

131

132

Muddy Fork

JODY'S BRIDGE

133

1270

134

LA WIS WIS C.G.

Clear Fork

Ohanapecosh R.

135

To White Pass & Cayuse Pass

N

36

RIVER MILE	RIVER TIME	LEFT BANK	RAPIDS	RIGHT BANK	DESCRIPTION
	5	⚓			— Skate Creek Bridge
	2:00				
	55				
	50		●2		— Waves, good kayak playspot
	45			✗	— Riprap right
	40				
	35			〜	— Butter Creek right
	30	〜			
	25				
	20	〜			— Lake Creek left
	15				
	10		◗ ◗		
RM 130	5				
	1:00				
	55				
	50	〜			— Coal Creek left
	45		◗		
	40				
	35			〜	— Muddy Fork of the Cowlitz right
	30				
	25		◗		— Log blocks channel left of island
				⚓	— Jody's Bridge
	20				
	15	■	●2	■	— Headwalls, first right, then left
	10		●2		
	5	⚓	●2	〜	— Put-in at main La Wis Wis camp left
					— Ohanapecosh river right
RM 135	12:00				— Bridge over Clear Fork of the Cowlitz

2

Naches

Logged at - 2,400 cfs Cliffdell gauge
Recommended water level - 1,200 to 2,600 cfs
Best time - Late April to late June
Rating - Intermediate
Water level information - NOAA Tape (206) 526-8530
NOAA Information (206) 526-6087
Bureau of Reclam. (509) 575-5854
River mile - 43.4 to 17.6; 25.8 miles
Time - 3 hours, 56 minutes; 6.6 mph
Elevation - 2,485' to 1575'; 35' per mile

There are lots of fun class 2 rapids on the Naches

38

Sawmill Flat to Tieton River

The Naches derives its name from an Indian word meaning "plenty of water." While this is dry country, there is usually plenty of water in the Naches during the May and June boating season. The upper part of the river is in the Wenatchee National Forest in a canyon lined with basalt cliffs and pine-forested hillsides. The lower end of the run is in stark desert country, but the rapids become more exciting. The Naches often has sun and warm temperatures in May and June when the water levels are good.

Getting There

The Naches is about 19 miles northeast of Yakima, flowing parallel to State Route 410. From the Puget Sound area, take Route 410 over Cayuse and Chinook passes, checking pass conditions before you leave in the fall or spring. (Often the roads aren't cleared of snow until late April or May.) The State Department of Transportation, (206) 764-4097, can tell you what to expect.

Put-ins and Take-outs

If you'd like to put in at the beginning of the logged run, you can do it easily at the picnic area of the Sawmill Flat Campground. When you look up and see the nice class 2 rapid just above the picnic area, though, you may want to look for a vacant campsite farther upriver and put in there.

Another convenient put-in or take-out point is the Cottonwood Campground. Or, you may want to use the fairly easy put-in/take-out just downstream of the upper Nile bridge on the left bank. The turn-off to the bridge is about 5.5 miles below Cottonwood Campground and about 14 miles above the turnoff for US 12.

If you'd just like to run the Horseshoe Bend stretch, you can put in at a wide gravel turnout along the road just below the log bridge at river time 3:05. It is rough, but it's the only place available.

The bottom take-out is almost directly below the US 12 bridge over the river. To reach it, take a left off US 12 about 0.1 mile past the bridge as you head toward White Pass. You'll find yourself on a poor dirt road, and if you bear left as it branches, it'll take you back to the bridge.

Water Level

You'll get a good run on the Naches when the water is from 1,200 to 2,600 cfs on the Cliffdell gauge. Kayakers and canoeists may enjoy the run down to 1,000 cfs. You can run the river above 2,600 cfs, but there are likely to be few eddies.

Naches
Cliffdell Gauge
Recommend 1,200 to 2,600 cfs

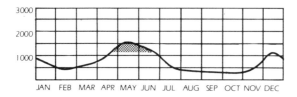

Special Hazards

Downed trees and **brush** sometimes block the smaller channels between islands, particularly in the section of the river from the lower Nile bridge to the class 3 rapid below it — about log time 2:40 to log time 2:54.

Scout the **dam** at log time 3:40 carefully. You'll be able to see it, and the building next to it, from the highway. You can scout, line or run the dam on the right, but remember that it's very dangerous to run any dam because the hydraulics can easily trap and hold anyone swimming in the river. Unless you're thoroughly familiar with river hydraulics and rescue techniques, do not run the dam, no matter how easy it looks to you.

There is a very dangerous **dam** about 0.25 mile below the take-out. Do not run it under any circumstances.

Scenery

In May and June, the area above the upper Nile bridge is often thick with wildflowers, and throughout the boating season, you'll enjoy the beautiful basalt cliffs that line much of the upper portion of the river. Don't be disappointed to find signs of civilization, how-ever; although the area is nearly all National Forest land, there are many private cabins and bridges across the river.

Spelunkers might want to take a side trip when they reach Boulder Cave picnic area on the right bank of the river, about log time 10 minutes. A 0.75-mile hike will take you up to Boulder Cave, fascinat-ing to explore because Devil Creek runs through it.

Below upper Nile bridge, the pine forests disappear as the land becomes drier. You'll leave behind the cliffs and notice the valley's widening. But, the trip ends with a bang. A spectacular canyon,

Bridges are the major landmarks on the river. (Leroy Gunstone photo)

narrow and dry, forms the Horseshoe Bend area near the end of the run, and it has the best rapids of the trip. Beyond, the land is so dry that you should watch for cactus at the take-out.

Camping

There's ample space at the Sawmill Flat and Cottonwood campgrounds, where it'll cost you about $4 per campsite to pitch a tent. Nearly all the land below Cottonwood Campground is privately owned, so don't camp there without permission from the landowner.

Rapids

You can see the most difficult rapids on the Naches from the highway, and it'll be easy for intermediate boaters to determine if this run suits their abilities. Intermediate boaters and canoeists should carefully study **Cottonwood** rapid, just below Cottonwood Campground, and the **Horseshoe Bend** area before running them. **Sticks and Stones** rapid at log time 2:53 is only listed as a class 3 because it's difficult to run some of the channels on the right side between the islands. You can identify it by the large boulders on the right, and intermediate boaters and canoeists should stop and scout it.

Canoeists should be able to handle the river above Horseshoe Bend easily but should be careful around Cottonwood rapid. Only expert canoeists are likely to make it through Horseshoe Bend without swamping and capsizing.

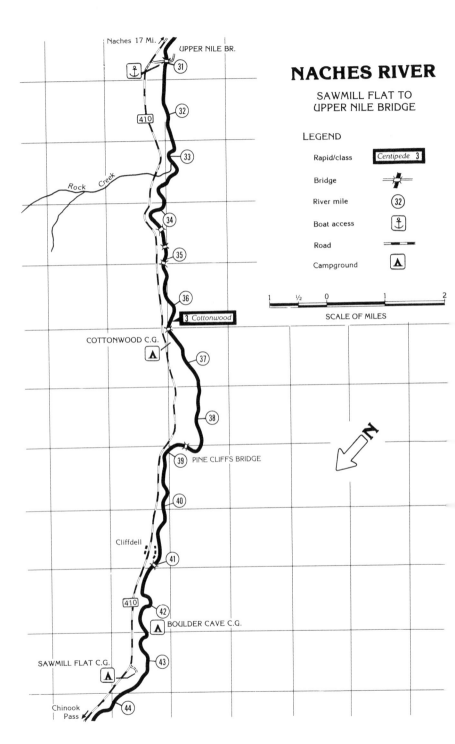

NACHES RIVER

SAWMILL FLAT TO
UPPER NILE BRIDGE

LEGEND

Rapid/class	Centipede 3
Bridge	
River mile	32
Boat access	
Road	
Campground	A

SCALE OF MILES

Naches 17 Mi.

UPPER NILE BR.

31

410

32

33

Rock Creek

34

35

36

3 Cottonwood

COTTONWOOD C.G.

37

38

39 PINE CLIFFS BRIDGE

40

Cliffdell

41

410

42

BOULDER CAVE C.G.

SAWMILL FLAT C.G.

43

Chinook Pass

44

N

RIVER MILE	RIVER TIME	LEFT BANK	RAPIDS	RIGHT BANK	DESCRIPTION
	2:00	⚓			—Upper Nile Road
	55		●2		
	50	▲▲	❘		
	45	▲▲		〽	—Spectacular cliffs right
	40	▲▲	●2 ❘		
	35	▲	●2		
	30	▲			
	25				—Log bridge
RM 35	20	▲		▲	—Red bridge / —Log bridge
	15	▲		▲▲	—Pinecliffs Bridge
	10	■		▲	—Gauging station, cable-car
	5	▲	●3		**Cottonwood**, scout left, run or line left / —Cottonwood Campground left
	1:00	▲▲	●2		
	55	▲▲	●2	▲	
	50		❘		
	45	▲▲			
	40			▲	
	35	▲		▲	
RM 40	30	▲▲	●2	〽	—Scenic cliffs right, then left / —Old bridge pier right
	25	▲▲	●2	▲	
	20	▲▲	●2		—Cliffdell Bridge
	15		❘		
	10	〽	●2 ●2		—Scenic cliffs left
	5		❘ ●2		—Gravel bar center-left
	12:00	▲	❘ ●2		—Sawmill Flat Campground

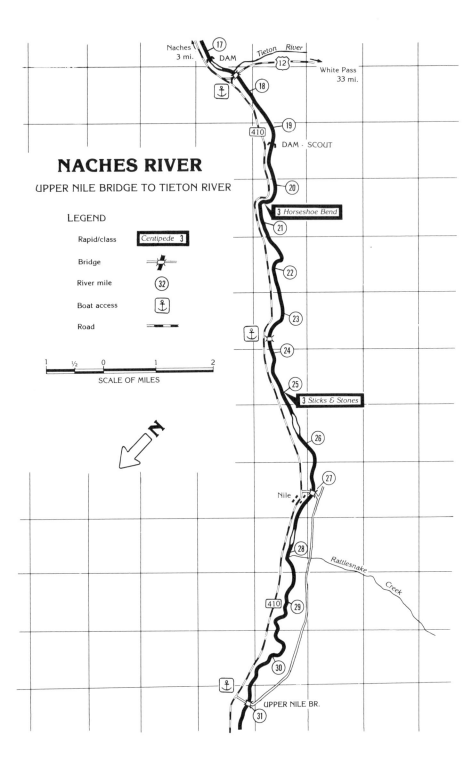

NACHES RIVER

UPPER NILE BRIDGE TO TIETON RIVER

LEGEND

Rapid/class	Centipede 3
Bridge	
River mile	32
Boat access	⚓
Road	

1 ½ 0 1 2
SCALE OF MILES

N

Naches
3 mi.

Tieton River

DAM

White Pass
33 mi.

17

12

18

⚓

19

410

DAM · SCOUT

20

3 Horseshoe Bend

21

22

23

⚓

24

25

3 Sticks & Stones

26

27

Nile

28

Rattlesnake Creek

410

29

30

⚓

UPPER NILE BR.

31

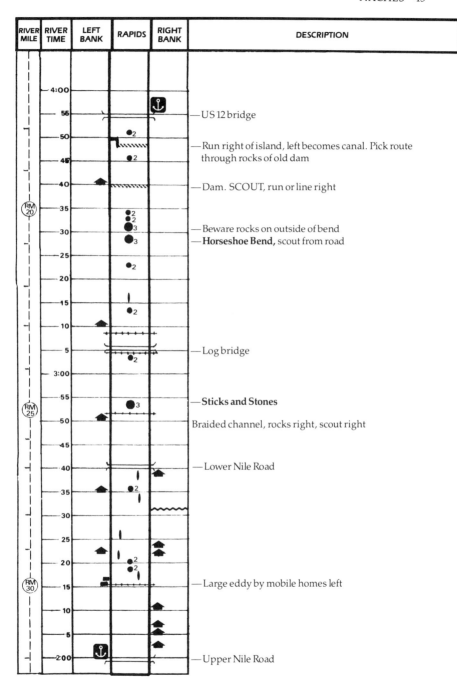

RIVER MILE	RIVER TIME	LEFT BANK	RAPIDS	RIGHT BANK	DESCRIPTION
	4:00				
	56				—US 12 bridge
	50		●2		
	45		●2		—Run right of island, left becomes canal. Pick route through rocks of old dam
	40				—Dam. SCOUT, run or line right
RM 20	35		●2 ●2		
	30		●3 ●3		—Beware rocks on outside of bend —**Horseshoe Bend,** scout from road
	25				
	20		●2		
	15				
	10		●2		
	5				—Log bridge
	3:00		●2		
	55		●3		**Sticks and Stones**
RM 25	50				Braided channel, rocks right, scout right
	45				
	40				—Lower Nile Road
	35		●2		
	30				
	25				
	20		●2 ●2		
RM 30	15				—Large eddy by mobile homes left
	10				
	5				
	2:00				—Upper Nile Road

Mt. Garfield is stunning from the put-in

3

Upper Middle Fork Snoqualmie

Logged at	-	1,300 cfs Middle Fork gauge
Recommended water level	-	1,200 to 3,500 cfs
Best time	-	April through early July
Rating	-	Intermediate
Water level information	-	NOAA Tape (206) 526-8530
		NOAA Information (206) 526-6087
River mile	-	64.3 to 57.1; 7.2 miles
Time	-	2 hours, 10 minutes; 3.3 mph
Elevation	-	1020' to 850'; 24' per mile

Taylor River to Concrete Bridge

The Upper Middle Fork provides a near wilderness trip within an hour's drive of the Seattle metropolitan area. With stunning mountain views and only one difficult rapid (which can be portaged with some difficulty), the Upper Middle allows intermediate boaters to get a feeling for the sort of experience that draws more advanced boaters to the few difficult overnight whitewater trips in the western United States.

The Forest Service wants to build a bridge across the river just below the mouth of the Pratt River so it can log the Pratt valley. To help stop this development of a prime scenic area, contact the Northwest Rivers Council (listed in Preface) and help make the Middle Fork a Wild & Scenic river.

Getting There

Take exit 34 (Edgwick Road) from I-90 and turn north under the freeway. On your left is Ken's Truck Stop. Continue about 0.2 mile north past Ken's and take a right at the T intersection. In about 0.9 mile the road divides and then rejoins again in 1.2 miles. Just beyond, the pavement ends. Continue a little over 3 miles more to the concrete bridge over the river.

Hold on in Rainy Creek Drop

Put-ins and Take-outs

To reach the take-out, continue about 0.25 mile past the bridge until the road crosses a culvert. About 200 yards beyond the culvert, take the unmarked dirt road, turning off to the right toward the river. About 0.1 mile down this road is the take-out. Although this take-out is on private land, it is open to the public.

An alternative take-out, which is at log time 1 hour, 28 minutes, can be reached by turning off toward the river on the unmarked dirt road that is 1.65 miles above the turn-off to the lower take-out. This is 0.55 mile above mile marker 6. This road goes in about 0.2 mile to a beach and requires a high-clearance vehicle. This take-out is also on private land, but the public is allowed to use it. Be wary of parking your vehicle on the "beach." Rapidly rising water can flood these sand and gravel bars.

To reach the put-in, continue on up Forest Service 56 road along the north side of the Middle Fork. About 5 miles above the lower take-out (or 3.5 above the upper take-out) Forest Service 210 road turns off to the left. Check your odometer at the 210 road sign, because the put-in is at the end of a 50-foot unmarked dirt road turning off toward the river just under 1 mile from this sign.

Water Level

You can scrape down the Upper Middle with as little as 800 cfs, but it's much more enjoyable with at least 1,200. Above 3,500 cfs the river approaches flood stage and most of the eddies are gone.

Upper Middle Fork Snoqualmie
Middle Fork Gauge
Recommend 1,200 to 3,500 cfs

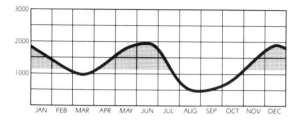

Special Hazards
Keep a sharp eye out for **logs** blocking the channel.

Scenery
On a clear day the scenery is outstanding. There are breath-taking views of Mt. Garfield above the put-in (between the Upper Middle and the Taylor rivers), Preacher Mountain and Russian Butte to the south and Green Mountain to the north. The Pratt River valley is revealed as a dramatic cleft between Preacher Mountain and Russian Butte in the middle of the run. Both the Upper Middle and the Middle Middle should be given Scenic river status in our federal Wild & Scenic Rivers System.

Camping
The only designated campground along the Middle Fork is oper-ated by the state's Department of Natural Resources at Mine Creek, a couple of miles below the take-out (see Chapter 12). However, people are welcome to camp anywhere on national forest land — at the put-in, for example. This trip could be combined with the Middle Middle (see Chapter 12) for an overnight trip, so several potential riverside campsites are marked on the log.

Rapids
Most of the rapids on the Upper Middle are straightforward class 2 drops. **Rainy Creek Drop,** however, has some good-sized waves and ends in a headwall. It can be portaged (with some difficulty) on the right bank. The bank is steep and rocky, but there is a very nice eddy to put in below the drop. Watch for the river plunging down out of sight toward the left bank as the sign for this rapid.

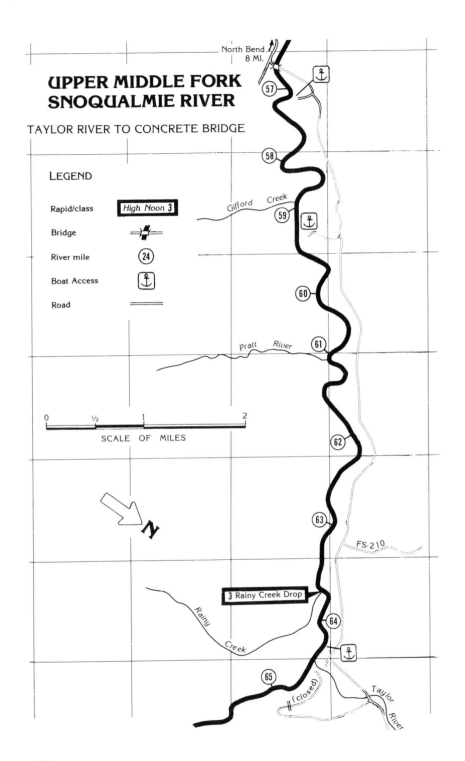

UPPER MIDDLE FORK SNOQUALMIE RIVER

TAYLOR RIVER TO CONCRETE BRIDGE

North Bend
8 MI.

LEGEND

Rapid/class	High Noon 3
Bridge	
River mile	24
Boat Access	
Road	

SCALE OF MILES
0   ½   1   2

N

Gifford Creek

Pratt River

FS-210

3 Rainy Creek Drop

Rainy Creek

(closed)

Taylor River

RIVER MILE	RIVER TIME	LEFT BANK	RAPIDS	RIGHT BANK	DESCRIPTION
			●2		Take-out right at time 2 hours, 10 minutes
	2:00				
	55				—Eroding clay bluffs right
	50		●2		
	45		*		—Large rock right
	40				—Eroding clay bluffs right
	35				—Gifford Creek left
	30		●2		
	25		●2	⚓	
RM 60	20				
	15	*			—Large rock left
	10				—Bridge pilings left
	5		●2		
	1:00				—Pratt River left
	55		●2		
	50		●2		
	45		●2		
	40		●2		
	35				
	30		●2		
	25		●2		—Sandy beach left
	20		●2		
	15		●2		
	10		●3		—**Rainy Creek Drop,** Rainy Creek left
	5		●2		
	12:00			⚓	

There are breath-taking mountain views from the Upper Sauk. (Keith Gunnar photo)

4

Upper Sauk

Logged at -	7,500 cfs Sauk gauge
Recommended water level -	5,500 to 12,000 cfs
Best time -	May to early July
Rating -	Intermediate
Water level information -	NOAA Tape (206) 526-8530
	NOAA Information (206) 526-6087
River mile -	40 to 31.7; 8.3 miles
Time -	2 hours, 4 minutes; 4.0 mph
Elevation -	1,125' to 900'; 27' per mile

Bedal Campground to White Chuck

Running through the thick forest of western Washington, the Sauk River offers both exciting paddling and marvelous scenery. The nearby crags of the Cascades are snow covered most of the year, and wildlife is often present. You are likely to see deer and waterfowl and perhaps an occasional otter or bear. The Sauk is protected as a scenic river under the federal Wild & Scenic Rivers Act.

Getting There

The best route to the upper Sauk is through Darrington, about 65 miles northeast of Seattle on State Route 530. To reach the new section of the Mountain Loop Highway heading south out of town to the Upper Sauk, go one block east of the 90-degree bend in the main road in Darrington, turn right and then, after several blocks, left at a T intersection. Follow the signs to "Mountain Loop Highway, Granite Falls." About 8.5 miles south of Darrington, the road crosses the Sauk just above the mouth of the White Chuck.

Put-ins and Take-outs

To reach the take-out, turn left, off the Mountain Loop Highway, about 200 yards after crossing the Sauk. You will cross the White Chuck and reach the river access site just below the mouth of the White Chuck.

To avoid running Rocky Road, the most difficult rapid at the end of the trip, park at the trailhead for the Beaver Lake Trail. This trailhead is up a short road that runs up the Sauk opposite the turnoff to the access site below the White Chuck. The trail runs along an abandoned road right-of-way next to the river for several hundred yards. The riverbank is steep but provides a take-out for those who don't mind carrying their boats some distance.

To reach the put-in, continue up the Mountain Loop Highway, which soon becomes a one-lane gravel road. About 8 miles up the road, turn right into Bedal Campground and reach the river through one of the campsites.

Water Level

Although kayakers or canoeists might be able to run the river at 4,000 cfs on the Sauk gauge, 5,500 cfs is about the minimum flow necessary for rafts. The maximum recommended flow is 12,000 cfs on the Sauk gauge. Above this level the river approaches flood stage and there are very few eddies. The best water levels for the trip are found from May through July. Later in the summer the river is likely to be low. Pay close attention to the effects of the weather upon the water level. A hot day or a good rain can cause the Sauk to rise exceptionally fast and make a day-old gauge reading completely inaccurate.

The river discharge levels on the Sauk gauge are much larger than what is actually present in the Upper Sauk. The gauge is located below the entrance of both the White Chuck and the Suiattle rivers on the Sauk. The percentage of water shown on the Sauk gauge that is actually flowing in the Upper Sauk varies by month as follows:

May	June	July	August
29%	27%	24%	20%

Upper Sauk
Sauk Gauge
Recommend 5,500 to 12,000 cfs

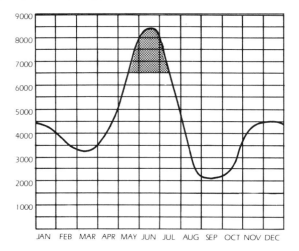

Special Hazards

Logjams are a great hazard on the Upper Sauk. Recently there have been logs completely crossing the river in at least one place every year. These logs are often left by high water at a height that allows the boater to pass underneath them, but they present a very serious hazard.

Scenery

The forest lining the riverbanks is untouched, and the views of the mountain peaks are some of the most stunning ones you'll see on any river. The water is a clear green, and the rocks of the riverbed can be clearly seen as you drift above them. You can see salmon and steelhead spawning here in July and August.

Camping

There are Forest Service campgrounds at the put-in and at Clear Creek, downstream along the Middle Sauk.

Rapids

The most difficult rapid on the trip is right at the end. **Rocky Road** can be viewed from the bridge across the Sauk just above the White Chuck. If you are an intermediate boater, you should inspect the rapid before your trip to determine if it is suitable for you. Generally the most exciting rapids are at the beginning and the end of the trip with a scenic float in-between. This river should be canoed only by experts who can avoid being swamped in the rapids at the beginning and the end of the trip.

Rocky Road *provides an exciting end to the trip*

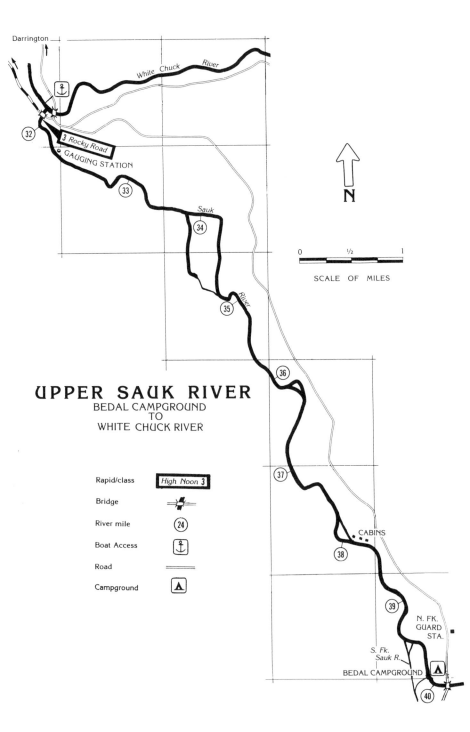

Darrington

White Chuck River

⚓

32

3 Rocky Road

GAUGING STATION

33

Sauk

34

N

0   ½   1

SCALE OF MILES

River

35

36

UPPER SAUK RIVER
BEDAL CAMPGROUND
TO
WHITE CHUCK RIVER

37

Rapid/class	High Noon 3
Bridge	✈
River mile	24
Boat Access	⚓
Road	=
Campground	▲

CABINS

38

39

N. FK. GUARD STA.

S. Fk. Sauk R.

BEDAL CAMPGROUND

▲

40

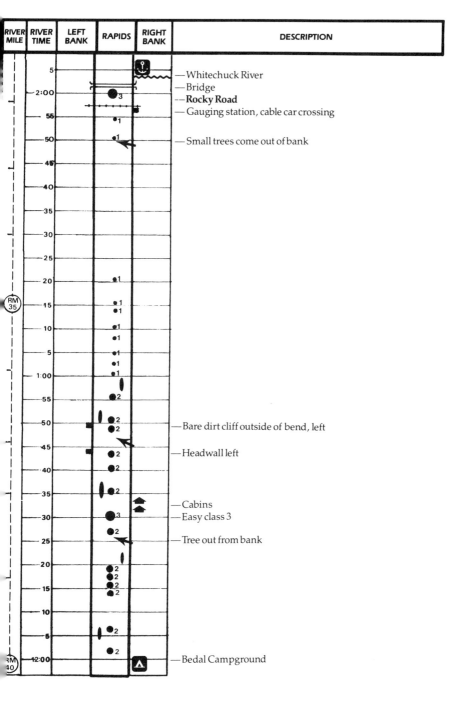

RIVER MILE	RIVER TIME	LEFT BANK	RAPIDS	RIGHT BANK	DESCRIPTION
	5				—Whitechuck River
	2:00		3		—Bridge
					--**Rocky Road**
	55		1		—Gauging station, cable car crossing
	50		1		—Small trees come out of bank
	45				
	40				
	35				
	30				
	25				
	20		1		
	15		1		
			1		
	10		1		
			1		
	5		1		
			1		
	1:00		1		
	55		2		
	50		2		—Bare dirt cliff outside of bend, left
			2		
	45		2		—Headwall left
	40		2		
	35		2		
					—Cabins
	30		3		—Easy class 3
			2		
	25				—Tree out from bank
	20				
			2		
	15		2		
			2 2		
	10				
	5		2		
			2		
	12:00				—Bedal Campground

5

Skagit

Logged at -	2,500 cfs Newhalem gauge
Recommended water level -	1,500 to 5,500 cfs
Best time -	August to October
Rating -	Intermediate
Water level information -	NOAA Tape (206) 526-8530
	NOAA Information (206) 526-6087
River mile -	92.8 to 83.9; 8.9 miles
Time -	2 hours, 8 minutes; 4.2 mph
Elevation -	473' to 355'; 13' per mile

Goodell Creek to Copper Creek

The Skagit River area is full of wonders. Paddle the river in early fall and you'll see salmon spawning. Paddle it during the winter months and you'll often be treated to the sight of bald eagles. Although the Skagit is dam controlled (by Seattle City Light's Ross, Diablo and Gorge dams), the river and surrounding area have remained so pristine that they are part of a national recreation area (NRA) attached to North Cascades National Park. The NRA does not prohibit dam construction, however, and Seattle City Light's proposed Copper Creek dam would turn this whole run into a reservoir. This section of the Skagit should be added to the federal Wild & Scenic Rivers system (joining the rest of the river below Bacon Creek) so that it remains free flowing.

Permits for the river are self-issued at the Goodell Creek Campground (the put-in). The National Park Service ranger at Marblemount can answer questions about the permits.

Getting There

The Skagit is paralleled by State Route 20 (the North Cascades Highway).

Put-ins and Take-outs

The put-in is at Goodell Campground, near the Seattle City Light

You will encounter much quiet beauty while drifting on the Skagit.
(Leroy Gunstone photo)

town of Newhalem (a corruption of the Indian word meaning "goat snare"). There's a steep take-out beside a wide turnout along the highway, about 2 miles above Bacon Creek. If you have lightweight boats, you may want to take out here, as it's located at the end of the whitewater. The best take-out is at the end of Copper Creek Road, which leaves the main highway 0.9 mile east of Bacon Creek Bridge, just before a yellow state highway sign. Turn right on the dirt road and go 0.2 mile to the riverbank.

Water Level

This section of the Skagit is nearly always runnable because it's regulated by dams. However, you might scrape your raft on the rocks if

There are fine views from the Skagit

you run at levels below 1,500 cfs on the Newhalem gauge. A maximum level of 5,500 cfs is recommended because above that point there are few eddies, and the hydraulics on the S curves become very powerful.

Keep in mind that Ross Dam is there to produce electricity. Thus, discharge from the dam will be higher during week days and peak electricity demand periods. Water levels will drop when the demand for power drops.

Skagit
Newhalem Gauge
Recommend 1,500 to 5,500 cfs

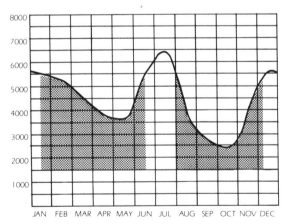

Special Hazards

None.

Scenery

Views of the nearby Cascades and abundant wildlife are the primary attractions of this trip from Goodell Creek Campground until log time 1:25. You'll see high, jagged peaks and deer, coyotes, foxes and racoons that live in the surrounding forest. You may also see an occasional bear, beaver or otter, and geese, ducks and trout are present almost all year.

Camping

If all the campsites at Goodell Creek Campground (the put-in) are taken, try Newhalem Campground, on the south side of the river, across the bridge at Newhalem. It has 129 sites and is rarely full. Camping along the river is prohibited.

Rapids

Much of the river is considered class 1 to 2. But at **Shovel Spur** (the Portage or S-bends) the whitewater becomes more exciting; that rapid is considered class 3 at low to moderate levels, class 4 at higher levels.

You'll approach Shovel Spur at log time 1:25. You can scout the entire rapid from State Route 20, and intermediate boaters should scout the rapid before putting in to see if they have the skills to run it. (The highway is above the riverbank, so you'll have a bird's-eye view of the rapid.)

The only eddies in this stretch of the river are near the left bank. Because the drops are on left bends in the river, you'll want to scout them from the left bank. Generally, you can run them by starting right, then moving to the center so you won't be driven into the right bank.

Shovel Spur *is the whitewater highlight of the trip. (Kevin O'Brien photo)*

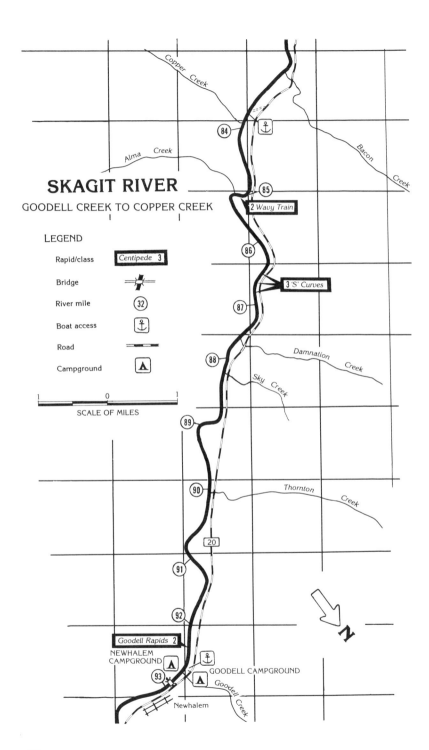

SKAGIT RIVER

GOODELL CREEK TO COPPER CREEK

Copper Creek

Alma Creek

Bacon Creek

84

85

2 Wavy Train

86

3 'S' Curves

87

Damnation Creek

88

Sky Creek

89

90

Thornton Creek

20

91

92

Goodell Rapids 2

NEWHALEM
CAMPGROUND

93

GOODELL CAMPGROUND

Goodell Creek

Newhalem

N

LEGEND

Rapid/class	Centipede 3
Bridge	
River mile	32
Boat access	
Road	
Campground	

0

SCALE OF MILES

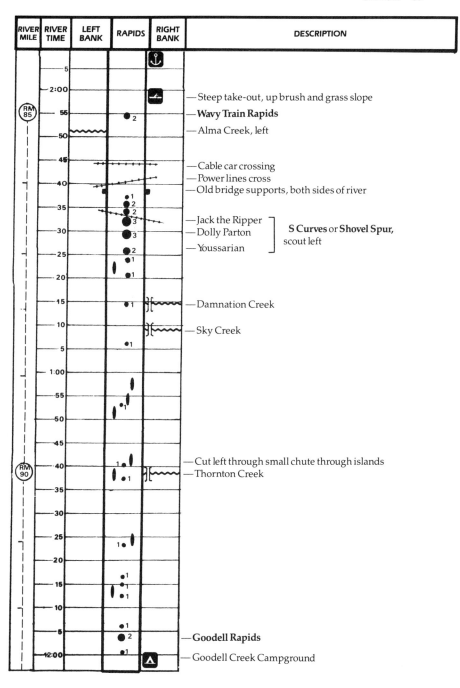

RIVER MILE	RIVER TIME	LEFT BANK	RAPIDS	RIGHT BANK	DESCRIPTION

— Steep take-out, up brush and grass slope
— **Wavy Train Rapids**
— Alma Creek, left

— Cable car crossing
— Power lines cross
— Old bridge supports, both sides of river

— Jack the Ripper
— Dolly Parton
— Youssarian

S Curves or **Shovel Spur,** scout left

— Damnation Creek

— Sky Creek

— Cut left through small chute through islands
— Thornton Creek

— **Goodell Rapids**
— Goodell Creek Campground

6

Suiattle

Logged at - 5,700 cfs Sauk gauge
Recommended water level - 2,500 to 9,000 cfs
Best time - July and August
Rating - Advanced
Water level information - NOAA Tape (206) 526-8530
NOAA Information (206) 526-6087
River mile - 11.7 to (Sauk River) 12.4; 12.7 miles
Time - 2 hours, 19 minutes; 5.5 mph
Elevation - 750' to 365'; 30' per mile

There's lots of excitement in Porcupine

Rat Trap Bridge to Sauk River Bridge

The Suiattle River will provide you with one of the best wilderness experiences on a western Washington river. Although there is evidence of logging on the surrounding ridges, the banks are thickly forested and there are no other signs of civilization until you reach the take-out. The river is protected as a scenic river under the federal Wild & Scenic Rivers Act and is a good place to spot deer, waterfowl and even an occasional bear. It is the traditional home of the Suiattle Indian tribe, and there is an Indian cemetery not far from the river a few miles upstream from the put-in.

The river is largely fed by glaciers on the north and east sides of Glacier Peak. Its milky water is often runnable through August and early September when other rivers are too low. The milky appearance of the Suiattle is the result of glacier flour. As the glacier grinds against rock formations, the ice wears the rock down to a fine powder. When the glacier melts, the rock powder flows into local streams and rivers.

Only expert open canoeists would be able to run the Suiattle. Even they should wait for a warm day because they are likely to be swamped frequently.

Getting There

The Suiattle flows into the Sauk River a few miles north of the town of Darrington. Darrington is about 65 miles northeast of Seattle on State Route 530. To reach the river, drive north out of Darrington toward Rockport.

Put-ins and Take-outs

You'll reach the take-out first, so you may wish to drop a car off there. It is on the right side of the bridge over the Sauk river, about 8 miles up the road from Darrington. (Alternative take-out is along the road just 0.5 mile south of the bridge, opposite the mouth of the Suiattle. There is a large dirt turnout there.)

To reach the put-in, continue on the highway away from Darrington. About 200 yards from the east end of the bridge over the Sauk, the main road bends to the left while a smaller paved road continues straight ahead. Go straight ahead on this road about 12 miles to Rat Trap Bridge. The road is generally well away from the river through the forest. It is paved all the way to Rat Trap Bridge with the exception of a couple of short gravel sections.

Water Level

The only gauge from which you can get a current reading is on the Sauk River, below the confluence of the Sauk and Suiattle. The Suiattle is best run between 2,500 cfs and 9,000 cfs on the Sauk gauge. It can be run at higher levels, but many of the rapids are washed out. Also, at higher levels you will find a considerable amount of debris floating down the river. At levels below 2,500 cfs it can be run in kayaks but is too low for rafts.

Suiattle
Sauk Gauge
Recommend 2,500 to 9,000 cfs

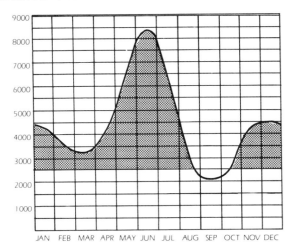

Special Hazards

The Suiattle is a young river that continually eats away at and changes its silt and clay banks. As the banks are eroded, trees and debris fall into the river, creating frequent logjams. The **logjams** can (and do) change from year to year and can go completely across the river. They present a severe hazard to boaters. Being forced against and underneath a sweeper will likely kill you.

The other principal danger is the **metal remains** of a bridge pier at log time 23 minutes. Stay well left.

In some years, commercial rafters have put in above Rat Trap Bridge, about 3 miles farther up the river at approximately river mile 15.4. In many recent years, however, the river has been completely blocked below this put-in by logjams 200 to 300 feet long. This section of the river should be completely scouted prior to attempting to run it. It is reported to be about as hard as the section covered by the following log.

The river has been run all the way from the end of the road at Sulphur Creek Campground down. The upper section is approximately 11 miles (Sulphur Creek Campground is near river mile 26.5) of very swift water. The rapids are not very difficult (class 3) but are nearly constant, with the water averaging about 12 to 15 miles per hour. There are lots of logjams (recently 8 logjams completely blocked the river), and getting out of the river is difficult due to the speed of the water and the lack of eddies. NO ONE should undertake a raft trip on this section of the river without first having it scouted by an expert kayaker. It is almost impossible to scout the river from the road because the two are usually separated by several hundred yards of thick forest and brush.

Scenery

You will have many beautiful views of natural forest with mountains in the background. There are almost no signs of civilization from the put-in to the take-out.

Camping

There are three Forest Service campgrounds within a 12-mile drive up the Suiattle from the put-in. The campgrounds at Buck Creek and Sulphur Creek are good-sized, while the one at Downey Creek is quite small. No fee is charged.

Rapids

Hurricane rapid at log time 51 minutes is the most difficult stretch of rapids and demands both good river-reading skills and control of the boat to avoid the numerous holes in the rapid. You can scout it from a gravel bar on the left bank, but landing is difficult as there is no eddy. You will reach Hurricane not long after passing Big Creek — a very noticeable large creek of clear water entering on the right. After a couple of bends in the river, you will see a gray, clay wall on the outside of a left bend in the river. Following that is a class 2 rapid and, around the next bend, Hurricane. It begins at a right bend in the river and has two drops with about 100 feet of fast water between them.

The other rapids are straightforward and, though many are exciting, they can easily be read from the boat by any experienced river runner.

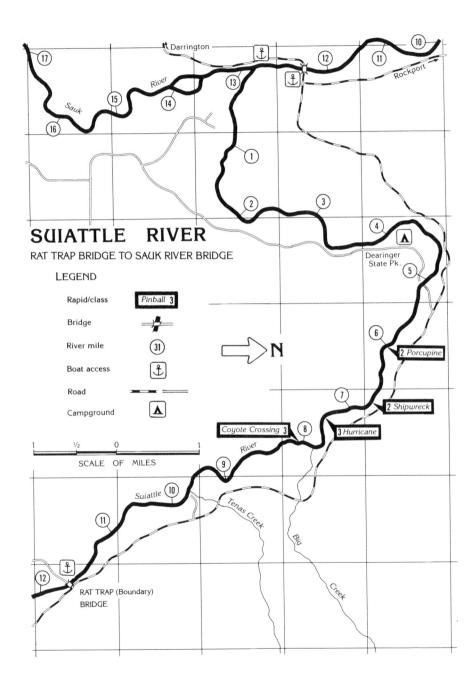

SUIATTLE RIVER

RAT TRAP BRIDGE TO SAUK RIVER BRIDGE

LEGEND

Rapid/class	**Pinball** **3**
Bridge	
River mile	㉛
Boat access	⚓
Road	
Campground	▲

⇨ **N**

Darrington

Sauk River

Rockport

Dearinger State Pk.

2 Porcupine

2 Shipwreck

3 Hurricane

Coyote Crossing **3**

River

Suiattle

Tenas Creek

Big Creek

RAT TRAP (Boundary)
BRIDGE

```
1        ½        0                 1
   SCALE   OF   MILES
```

RIVER MILE	RIVER TIME	LEFT BANK	RAPIDS	RIGHT BANK	DESCRIPTION
	2:00				— Stay right, away from logs
	55				
	50				— Huge logjam left
	45				— More water right
	40				— Large hole, middle top of drop
					— Large rock with white stripes
	35				
	30				
	25				— Easy class 3
	20				— Dearinger State Park, left
RM 5	15				
	10				
	5				— **Porcupine,** rocks on left
	1:00				— Headwall, left bank
					— Big fun waves
	55				— **Shipwreck,** big waves
	50				— **Hurricane Rapids** (Machine Gun), scout left
	45				— Gray wall, right bank
					— Big Creek
	40				— **Coyote Crossing**
					— Exposed gray rock, right
	35				
	30				
	25				— Tenas Creek
RM 10	20				— Destroyed bridge, run left to avoid sharp metal on remainder of pier
	15				— Difficult maneuvering to avoid logjams
	10				— Gray rock, left bank
					— Rock, center left
	5				— Run left of hole in center to hit big waves
	12:00				— Rat Trap (Boundary) Bridge

Heavy forest lines the Suiattle

The middle section of the run has nearly constant action

RIVER MILE	RIVER TIME	LEFT BANK	RAPIDS	RIGHT BANK	DESCRIPTION
	4:00				
	55				
	50				
	45				
	40				
	35				
	30				
	25				
	20				
	15				
	10				
	5				
	3:00				
	55				
	50				
	45				
	40				
	35				
	30				
	25				
	20				—Sauk River Bridge
	15	⚓		⚓	—Confluence with Sauk River
	10				
	5		•1		—Cut bank, right
	2:00				

7

Wenatchee

Logged at - 6,700 cfs Peshastin gauge
Recommended water level - 4,000 to 15,000 cfs
Best time - May to mid-July
Rating - Advanced
Water level information - NOAA Tape (206) 526-8530
NOAA Information (206) 526-6087
River mile - 24.6 to 5.8; 18.8 miles
Time - 3 hours, 30 minutes; 5.4 mph
Elevation - 1,100' to 680'; 22' per mile

Leavenworth to Monitor

The Wenatchee is a snow-fed river running off the east side of the North Cascades. It is probably the most popular and frequently run river in Washington. After the winter snowpack has melted and pooled in Lake Wenatchee, the river thunders through Tumwater Canyon and exits near Leavenworth. The Indians fished for salmon and steelhead near present-day Leavenworth, and "Wenatchee" comes from their name for the river which means "river flowing from canyon." Boaters with an instinct for survival pass up the class 4 to 6 rapids of Tumwater Canyon and put in at Leavenworth.

Getting There
The Wenatchee is paralleled by US 2 from Leavenworth to Monitor.

Put-ins and Take-outs
The old put-in near the Icicle Creek Road bridge has been closed because boaters using the riverbank as a restroom posed a health hazard to Leavenworth, which has its water supply intake near there. The log still starts at the bridge to orient those who are familiar with

In years past, a rodeo, with a hole-riding competition, has been held on the Wenatchee

that area, but the first put-in is downstream, opposite Leavenworth at log time 28 minutes.

To get to the new put-in, turn off US 2 just east of the bridge over the river, east of Leavenworth. The road goes west, up the Wenatchee. In about 0.8 mile, turn right (off the outside of a bend in the road) onto a dirt road 0.1 mile to the river. This unimproved boat ramp site is managed by Leavenworth and may be used only by noncommercial boaters. Note that this put-in gives you barely 12 minutes to warm up before you are into Boulder Bend — the most difficult rapid on this stretch of river.

The old put-in near Peshastin (Indian for "wide-bottom canyon") along the highway has also been closed. The danger created by cars pulling off and on the highway along the curve necessitated this closure. There is still an access site in the Peshastin area, however. The state Department of Wildlife has a rough boat ramp on School Street in Peshastin. Cross the bridge from US 2 to Peshastin and turn right on School Street. Go 0.3 mile to the ramp on the north side of the river at log time 1 hour, 36 minutes. A Department of Wildlife conservation license is needed to use this access site (see Introduction).

The upper take-out is provided by Cashmere, just below the Division Street Bridge. Parking and a changing area are available; you can reach it by turning off Division Street, which intersects US 2.

The lower take-out is at Monitor (named for the Union ironclad in the Civil War) at the Department of Wildlife's river access site (conservation license required). To reach the access site, turn off US 2 at the Monitor Bridge. The take-out is just upstream from the bridge on the right bank.

Water Level

The Wenatchee is runnable at a wide range of water levels. About 3,000 cfs is needed for larger rafts (though the recommended 4,000 cfs is more enjoyable), but small rafts and kayaks can run it on as little as 1,500 cfs. It can be run in open canoes at levels below 3,000 cfs, although only experts are likely to avoid swamping at levels above 1,800 cfs in Boulder Bend, Rock 'n Roll and Drunkard's Drop.

Above 10,000 cfs many rocks are covered and the river channel becomes less interesting, but the powerful hydraulics can make for a very exciting ride. Although water moves swiftly at high levels, it is reasonably safe at all levels below 20,000 cfs. The run is slower and distinctly less exciting below 6,000 cfs and you may wish to use the lower put-in at Peshastin at these levels.

Wenatchee
Peshastin Gauge
Recommend 4,000 to 15,000 cfs

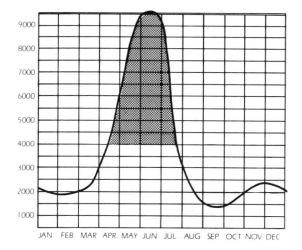

Special Hazards

PORTAGE the irrigation **dam** at Dryden, a little below Rock 'n Roll. The dam forms a small pool, and it is easy to take out on the right bank and carry around on the path cleared for portaging. The dam used to be runnable at moderate water levels but was reconstructed over the 1986-87 winter and is now a drowning machine. It creates a uniform wave breaking upstream all the way across the river. The water on the surface moves upstream toward the face of the dam. It is very difficult for people caught in this hydraulic to escape; they will likely recirculate until they drown. When putting back into the river below the dam, be sure to get well below the boil line. The current is stronger than it looks and can pull a boat back upriver into the dam.

Scenery

There are some nice bluffs and apple orchards along the Wenatchee, but other than the view of the mountains at the beginning of the trip, you're here for the whitewater, not the scenery. Civilization is much in evidence on this trip, and in many places there is junk scattered along the riverbank.

Camping

Nearly all the land along the river is privately owned, so don't camp along the river except at Wenatchee County Park (the take-out) or the

There's big water on the Wenatchee during spring runoff. (Kevin O'Brien photo)

KOA campground near Leavenworth. A fee is charged for the use of these campgrounds. To avoid paying a fee, you must drive about 8 miles up Icicle Creek Road to the first of a series of Forest Service campgrounds.

Rapids

The first significant rapid you will reach after the put-in and also the most difficult on the Wenatchee is **Boulder Bend.** The rapid is upon you soon after the highway bridge. Boulder Bend consists of a right bend that shelves to the left (or outside) of the bend with a large rock formation in the middle. The formation is an obstacle below 8,000 to 9,000 cfs and a large hole above that level.

Scouting Boulder Bend is difficult. The only good landing places are on the left bank. Once a boat has landed on the left bank, however, the force of the water pushing toward the outside of the bend makes it almost impossible to ferry and run the right side of the rock formation. To preserve the option of running the right side (or inside of the bend) scout right. Scouting right is difficult, as there are no real eddies or landing places on the right bank; you must simply jump out and grab a boulder.

At water levels over 5,000 cfs it is possible to ferry to the right of the rock formation, running the inside of the bend, then dodging the rocks and running the waves below. You must run to the left of the rock formation at lower water levels because there will be insufficient water

Watch out for waves and holes in Snowblind. *(Kevin O'Brien photo)*

on the right; this run is very difficult due to the shelving to the left. The shelving forces the water to pour in from the right carrying you left toward the outside of the bend and many large rocks and holes. Thus, run right where possible.

The next major and longest (200-yard) rapid on the Wenatchee is **Rock 'n Roll.** This rapid contains Satan's Eyeball, a large hole that forms in the right center of the river at water levels from about 2,500 cfs up to about 12,000 cfs. You should scout by landing at the head of the island on the left (watch for a small flow of the river which goes off through boulders and brush on the left side of the island). It is necessary to push through brush, but by working your way down the island, the whole rapid can be scouted. Above 3,500 cfs, in addition to the Eyeball and another hole downstream to the left, the rapid consists of big waves, great fun for paddlers. Below 3,500 cfs rocks become increasingly evident, and below 2,500 cfs the rapid becomes a rock garden. Ferrying left of Satan's Eyeball becomes difficult over about 9,000 cfs as most of the water flows across the river toward the hole. The conservative run from 9,000 cfs to 12,000 cfs is to hug the right shore. Above 12,000 cfs Satan's Eyeball disappears and is replaced by an immense wave that can stand a 10-man raft on end. Hard paddling or rowing is necessary to avoid stalling on the wave.

Below the dam, you'll reach the third class 3 rapid, **Gorilla Falls,** under the highway bridge. The best run is near the right pier, away from rocks on the left.

Kayakers will find great surfing on the ledges at river mile 14.

Drunkard's Drop is the fourth significant rapid on the Wenatchee. It involves a substantial 3 to 4 foot drop but no other real obstacle other than its shallowness at lower water levels. The drop, however, is at an angle to the flow of the river so you will encounter waves hitting you at an angle from the right.

The rapid occurs right where the river turns upon encountering a sheer dirt bluff on the left side. At levels between 4,000 and 10,000 cfs a powerful eddy forms next to the bluffs on river left. Scouting can be done either right or left. Scouting river right allows you to walk downstream of the drop for additional inspection but is difficult at high water as the gravel bar on the right side is covered. When scouting, land far enough upriver to allow time for a ferry, if necessary, prior to entering the rapid.

The best raft approach is to swing far left, just above the drop, and go straight down the drop and toward the center of the river, hitting the waves head on. Attempting to cheat the drop on the right is often unsuccessful.

Person overboard in Suffocator! *(Kevin O'Brien photo)*

For smaller boats, the drop is actually most difficult at about 2,000 cfs as the first wave becomes a back-curler, creating a hole that extends all the way across the river. The back-curler is 2 to 3 feet high and will easily stop a small raft or flip a poorly handled kayak. At 2,500 cfs the back-curler turns into a smooth wave, while at 1,500 cfs the back-curler is too small to be a problem.

The last significant rapid on the river is **Snowblind.** The river tumbles over several rocks and ledges, creating waves and holes. Generally, it can be run down the center or left by threading around the holes.

Granny's Rapid is not considered class 3, because you can avoid it. The large waves of Annapurna and K-2, and the back-curler (Suffocator) can provide a lot of fun, however.

WENATCHEE RIVER

LEAVENWORTH TO DRYDEN

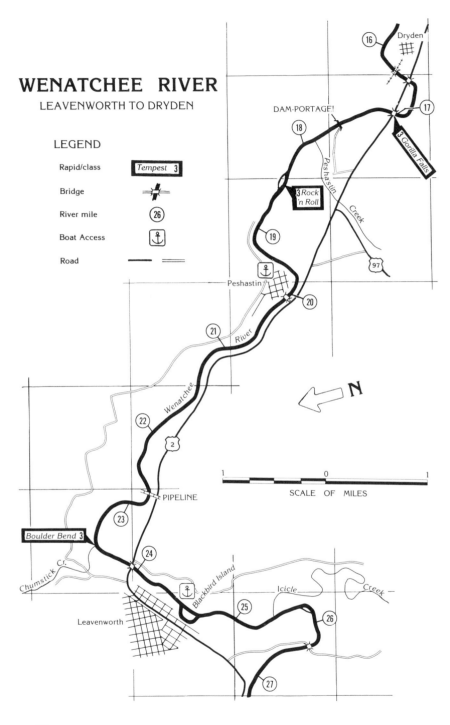

LEGEND

Rapid/class	*Tempest* 3
Bridge	
River mile	㉖
Boat Access	⚓
Road	

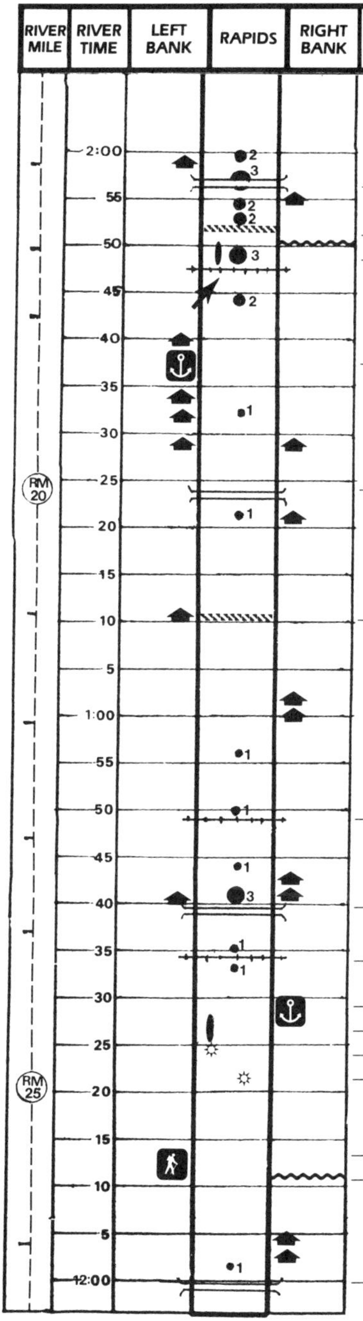

RIVER MILE	RIVER TIME	LEFT BANK	RAPIDS	RIGHT BANK	DESCRIPTION

—**Gorilla Falls,** under highway bridge; run close to right pillar

—Dam, PORTAGE; Peshastin Creek right

—**Rock 'n Roll,** scout left on island

—Dept. of Wildlife School St. access

—Peshastin Bridge

—Rock dam; run left at low water

—Pipe crossing

—**Boulder Bend** (Chumstick, Rock Garden, Hobo Gulch), scout right, run right

—Low water playspot, cable crossing

—East Leavenworth access

—Blackbird Island left

—Pilings left

—Pilings midstream

—Golf course left

—Icicle Creek

—Icicle Creek Road bridge

RM 20

RM 25

2:00

55

50

45

40

35

30

25

20

15

10

5

1:00

55

50

45

40

35

30

25

20

15

10

5

12:00

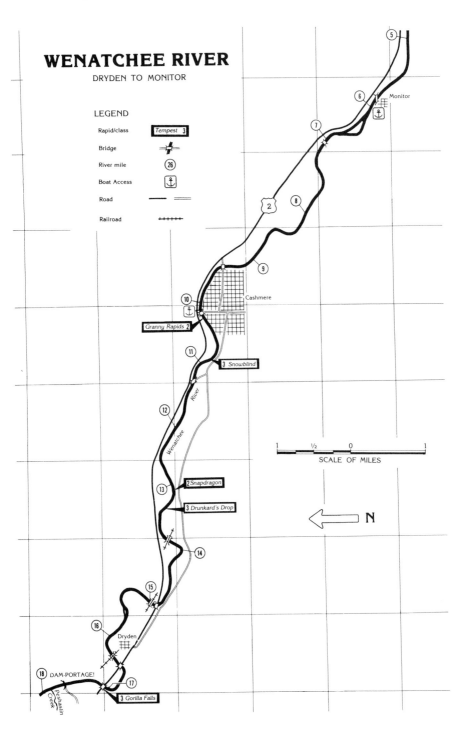

WENATCHEE RIVER

DRYDEN TO MONITOR

LEGEND

Rapid/class	Tempest 3
Bridge	
River mile	26
Boat Access	
Road	
Railroad	+++++

Monitor

Cashmere

Granny Rapids 2

3 Snowblind

Wenatchee River

SCALE OF MILES

N

2 Snapdragon

3 Drunkard's Drop

Dryden

DAM-PORTAGE!

Peshastin Creek

3 Gorilla Falls

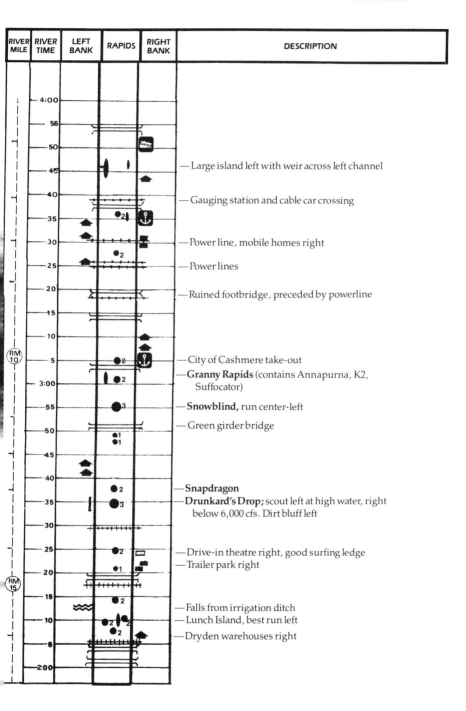

RIVER MILE	RIVER TIME	LEFT BANK	RAPIDS	RIGHT BANK	DESCRIPTION
	4:00				
	55				
	50				
	45				—Large island left with weir across left channel
	40				—Gauging station and cable car crossing
	35		•2		
	30				—Power line, mobile homes right
	25		•2		—Power lines
	20				—Ruined footbridge, preceded by powerline
	15				
	10				
RM 10	5		•2		—City of Cashmere take-out
	3:00		•2		—**Granny Rapids** (contains Annapurna, K2, Suffocator)
	55		•3		—**Snowblind,** run center-left
	50				—Green girder bridge
	45		•1 •1		
	40				
	35		•2 •3		—**Snapdragon**
					—**Drunkard's Drop;** scout left at high water, right below 6,000 cfs. Dirt bluff left
	30				
	25		•2		—Drive-in theatre right, good surfing ledge
	20		•1		—Trailer park right
RM 15	15		•2		—Falls from irrigation ditch
	10		•2 •2 •2		—Lunch Island, best run left
	5				—Dryden warehouses right
	2:00				

8

Tieton

Logged at - 1,700 cfs Rimrock gauge
Recommended water level - 1,000 to 2,200 cfs
Best time - September
Rating - Advanced
Water level information - NOAA Tape (206) 526-8530
NOAA Information (206) 526-6087
Bureau of Reclam. (509) 575-5854
River mile - 20.1 to 8.5; 11.6 miles
Time - 1 hour, 57 minutes; 5.9 mph
Elevation - 2,640' to 2,015'; 54' per mile

Rimrock to Windy Point

A pleasant way to cap a season of paddling is to make a September run of the high waters of the Tieton in sunny eastern Washington. The Tieton takes its name from an Indian word meaning "roaring water." A trip on the river will convince you that it's an appropriate name. The Tieton would make a fine addition to our federal Wild & Scenic Rivers system as a recreational river.

During most of the spring and summer, the federal Bureau of Reclamation, which operates Rimrock Dam, holds back the water of the Tieton. Irrigation water for the lower Yakima Valley is drawn from the Keechelus, Kachess and Cle Elum reservoirs farther up the Yakima River. In September, salmon and steelhead return to the Yakima to spawn, and the water level in the upper river has to be reduced so that the fish do not spawn in a portion of the riverbed that will be exposed when the water level is low during the winter.

To accommodate the fish, the water in the upper Yakima is dropped to winter levels in September, and the irrigation water needed in the lower Yakima Valley is drawn from the Tieton, which flows into the Naches and then into the Yakima near the city of Yakima, below the spawning beds. Thus, when the river comes up is determined by the fish, who are watched by fisheries biologists. In wet years, the Tieton

Lots of rocks stud the steep descent of the Tieton. (Alyce Daniels photo)

will reach runnable levels in June, when excess water is spilled into the river after the reservoir has been filled. But in most years, the Tieton only comes alive in September, when the fish spawn and the irrigation water roars down the river.

Getting There
US 12 runs along the Tieton between White Pass and Yakima, just west of prime apple orchard country.

Put-ins and Take-outs
Because the river is so swift, putting in and taking out are both difficult, as is rescue in the event of an upset. The run starts in a steep, pine-forested valley just below Tieton Dam. The upper put-in shown on the log is reached by turning off US 12 on an unmarked dirt road 0.65 mile below the Rimrock grocery. It is not easy to put in here because the river is lined with bushes.

An easier put-in is found at Hause Creek Campground at log time 18 minutes. The other campgrounds shown on the map and log can also be used for put-ins and take-outs, but landing is not easy as there are very few eddies.

Water Level
You can run the Tieton on 1,000 to 2,200 cfs on the Rimrock gauge. Be cautious at the higher levels, however, because lack of eddies makes rescues difficult. Kayaks and small inflatables can scrape down the river on about 700 cfs.

Tieton
Rimrock Gauge
Recommend 1,000 to 2,200 cfs

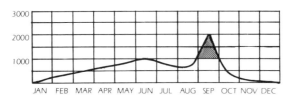

Special Hazards

PORTAGE the **dam** at log time 53 minutes. It's a straight drop of 3 to 6 feet with a powerful reversal below the right side, and you'll want to plan carefully to avoid it. A 1986-87 dam repair resulted in an even more vicious hydraulic below the structure. The dam is hidden 20 feet

Portage the dam! (Alyce Daniels photo)

past a sharp left bend in the river. Watch for the warning signs along the bank, and take the small channel between the two islands on the left. Otherwise, you may have a difficult, if not impossible, time reaching the left bank before you're swept over the drop. The eddy above the dam can easily fill up on crowded weekends. To make sure there is enough room for you to land, do *not* follow several other boats closely when approaching the dam.

The dam should be quickly and quietly portaged on the left bank. The gatekeeper and his family live right by the dam and this is their backyard. Do not relieve yourself in the bushes; there are facilities at the campgrounds. And do not go out on the footbridge which crosses the river over the dam; it is maintained exclusively for irrigation district work. Don't grab the electrical cable hanging under the bridge. And stay away from the irrigation canal intake on the right bank.

There are reportedly frequent **logjams** on the portion of the Tieton below the logged run and always the possibility of one on this section. Stay alert!

Scenery

The plant life changes dramatically as the river descends from approximately 2,650 feet at the put-in to 2,000 feet at the take-out. The valley becomes drier, and pine forests disappear, replaced by sage-covered hills and stark rock formations. In September, the only green remaining near the end of the run is right along the riverbed.

Camping

The Tieton is lined with U. S. Forest Service campgrounds, so camping is easy. But as always, the drive-in camps may be crowded and noisy. You will avoid the crowds, however, by camping after Labor Day. Hause Creek Campground is particularly large, but much of it is closed after September 15. You'll have to pay a fee to use all the campsites along the river.

Rapids

The Tieton is rated a class 2 to class 3 river. However, this run is actually more difficult than the class ranking indicates. The first 6 miles are very steep and the water moves very fast. The rapids are all short drops, and the class 3s earn their ratings more because rescues are difficult in those areas than because they're technically challenging. The rapids are nearly constant, the water swift with almost no eddies.

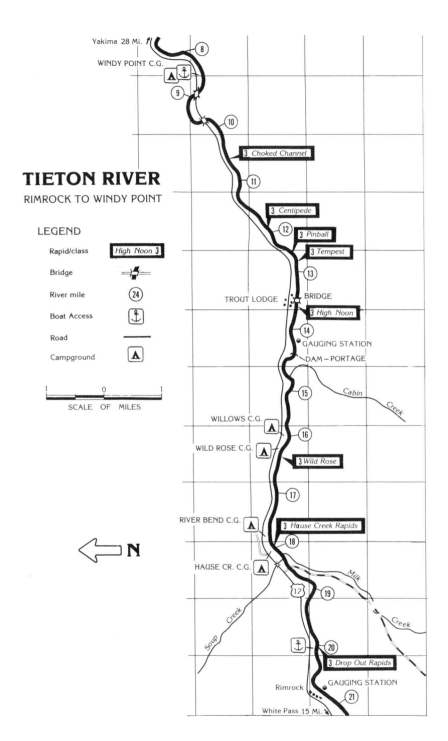

TIETON RIVER

RIMROCK TO WINDY POINT

Yakima 28 Mi.

⑧

WINDY POINT C.G.

⑨

⑩

3 Choked Channel

⑪

3 Centipede

⑫ 3 Pinball

3 Tempest

⑬

TROUT LODGE   BRIDGE

3 High Noon

⑭

GAUGING STATION

DAM – PORTAGE

⑮

Cabin Creek

WILLOWS C.G.

⑯

WILD ROSE C.G.

3 Wild Rose

⑰

RIVER BEND C.G.

3 Hause Creek Rapids

⑱

HAUSE CR. C.G.

12

⑲

Milk Creek

Soup Creek

⑳

3 Drop Out Rapids

Rimrock   GAUGING STATION

㉑

White Pass 15 Mi.

LEGEND

Rapid/class	High Noon 3
Bridge	
River mile	24
Boat Access	⚓
Road	
Campground	▲

1   0   1

SCALE   OF   MILES

← N

RIVER MILE	RIVER TIME	LEFT BANK	RAPIDS	RIGHT BANK	DESCRIPTION
	2:00				
	55	▲			—Windy Point Campground
	50		•2		—Highway bridge
			•2		—Old bridge abutment left
	45		•2 •2 •2	⇦	
	40		❙ • 2		—Highway bridge
RM 10	35		•2 •2		
	30		❙•3 ❙• 2		—**Choked channel**
	25	⇧ 🚂	•3 •3❙ •2		—No trees or brush between river and road on outside of bend, left
	20		• 2 •3		—**Centipede**
	15		•3 •3		—**Pinball**
	10		•3 •2 •2		—**Tempest** (Waffle)
	5		•2		
	1:00	⬆ ⬆	❙•3 * *		—**High Noon,** run far right, tough class 3
		⬆	•2 •2		—Conglomerate rocks
	55				
	50		❙❙	⊐	—Dam: PORTAGE left, rock wall right bank
RM 15	45	—	•2 •2 •2 •2 ✦		
	40		•2		—Rock with river debris, road sign left bank "171"
	35	▲	•2 •3 •3		—**Wild Rose Rapids,** Wild Rose campground, left
	30	⛰	•2		—Rock cliffs above road, left bank
	25	▲	•2 •2 * •2		—Conglomerate rock right
	20		•3 •2		—Sign "River Bend Campground" left
	15	▲	•2 •3		—**Hause Creek Rapids,** old bridge abutment left. Run far right. Hause Creek Campground left
	10	❙	•3 •2		—Two big fun waves
	5	—	•2 •2		—Rock culvert from under road, left bank
RM 20	12:00	⚓	•3 •3		—**Drop Out Rapids**
					—Rough put-in, no real eddy

North Fork Nooksack

Logged at - 700 cfs on North Fork gauge
Recommended water level - 600 to 1,600 cfs
Best time - May through October
Rating - Advanced
Water level information - NOAA Tape (206) 526-8530
NOAA Information (206) 526-6087
River mile - 59.3 to 51.5; 7.8 miles
Time - 1 hour, 40 minutes; 4.7 mph
Elevation - 970' to 555'; 53' per mile

Milky glacial water will challenge your river-reading skills

Douglas Fir Campground to Maple Falls

The North Fork of the Nooksack is fed by snow and ice on Mt. Baker and the North Cascades. It is named after the Indians who lived in the area and were known as the "mountain men." On clear days, there are spectacular views of Mt. Baker and the surrounding mountains. The trip begins in a narrow gorge with many class 3 rapids in quick succession.

Just above the put-in, across the highway from Douglas Fir Campground, is the Horseshoe Bend Interpretive Trail. If you take a short walk up this trail you will see very intense whitewater in a beautiful gorge. The most difficult of the drops are probably unrunnable in a raft and could be run only by a very skillful kayaker. The North Fork would make a fine addition to our national Wild & Scenic Rivers system.

Getting There

The North Fork of the Nooksack is paralleled by State Route 542, the Mt. Baker Highway. Take exit 255 from I-5, the Sunset Drive exit. Turn right and head first for Deming and then Maple Falls.

Put-ins and Take-outs

You'll get to the take-out first, so you may wish to drop a car off there. It is at the end of a very short dirt road just beyond mile marker 27, about 1.5 miles above Maple Falls. It is on private land and the owners have been kind enough to allow boaters to take out here. Please park only one shuttle vehicle here and leave the rest of your vehicles elsewhere. Don't leave any litter behind; if the property is abused, the owners may close it to boaters. The take-out is not easily spotted from the river; you may want to tie a flag to a tree so you don't miss it.

An intermediate put-in or take-out point is reached at the highway bridge over the river, about 2.5 miles below Glacier. A short dirt road turns off the downstream side of State Route 542, 50 yards northwest of the bridge over the river. The dirt road is steep, and often four-wheel drive is required in wet weather. Recently, the main channel of the river shifted away from the right bank in this area, and boats have to be dragged over a gravel bar to get them to and from the river.

The main put-in is at Douglas Fir Campground, about 2 miles upriver from Glacier and clearly marked on the highway. You should put in as far upstream in the campground as possible in order to have a short warm-up before hitting the class 3 rapids of the gorge. You may want to put in on the upstream (east) side of the highway on the right bank in order to avoid disturbing campers in the campground.

Water Level

Radio telemetry has recently been installed on the North Fork gauge, making current river-level readings available, so it is no longer necessary to calculate the North Fork's flow from the Deming gauge. The North Fork can be run from 600 cfs to 1,600 cfs, though care should be taken in the gorge at higher levels due to the swiftness of the water. Because of the large amount of glacial melt from Mt. Baker flowing into the North Fork, it is one of the few free-flowing rivers that is normally runnable in late August and September.

Nooksack
North Fork Gauge
Recommend 600 to 1,600 cfs

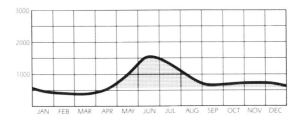

Special Hazards

Logs are a great hazard on the Nooksack and occasionally have completely blocked the channel; stay alert!

Scenery

The gorge that makes up the first part of this run is dark, narrow and dramatic. It is rock-choked and very scenic, with moss covering the banks and hanging from the trees. The end of the gorge is reached near the mouth of Glacier Creek, where the boater trades the beauty of the gorge for the wider view of the broadened river valley and the surrounding mountains. The channel begins to braid but still contains some interesting rapids, at least as far as the highway bridge. The whole trip is through a natural valley with few signs of civilization.

The beginning of the Nooksack run is in a very steep and narrow gorge

Camping

Campsites are available at Douglas Fir Campground — the put-in. There are other Forest Service campgrounds farther up State Route 542.

Rapids

The rapids at the beginning of the trip come fast and furious. You must be prepared to read and run many successive class 3 rapids without scouting. After Glacier Creek, the pace slackens, but you should watch carefully for logs across the river.

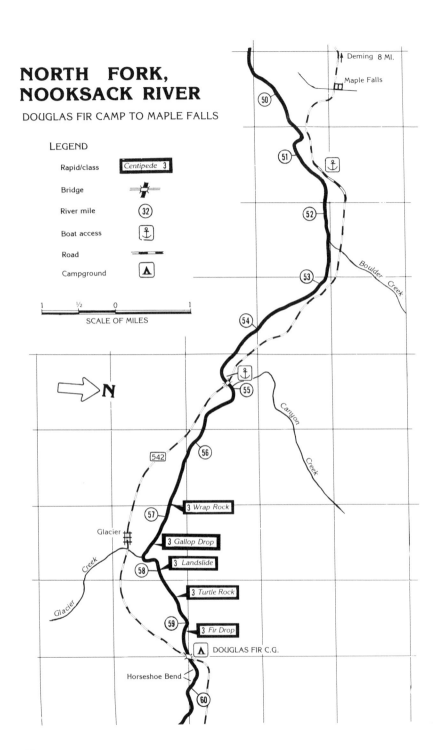

NORTH FORK, NOOKSACK RIVER

DOUGLAS FIR CAMP TO MAPLE FALLS

LEGEND

Rapid/class   Centipede 3

Bridge

River mile   32

Boat access   ⚓

Road

Campground   ⚑

SCALE OF MILES

N

Deming 8 MI.

Maple Falls

50

51

52

53

Boulder Creek

54

55

Canyon Creek

56

542

57

3 Wrap Rock

Glacier

3 Gallop Drop

58

3 Landslide

Glacier Creek

3 Turtle Rock

59

3 Fir Drop

⚑ DOUGLAS FIR C.G.

Horseshoe Bend

60

RIVER MILE	RIVER TIME	LEFT BANK	RAPIDS	RIGHT BANK	DESCRIPTION
	2:00				
	55				
	50				
	45				
	40		⚓		— Take-out on right of small right channel
	35				
	30			⬆	— Farm just visible over bar
	25		•2	)(	— Boulder Creek, bridge visible in distance
	20				
	15				
	10		| •2		— Fun waves
					— Beaver area right
	5				— Fun waves
	1:00		•2 / •2		— Fun waves
	55		•2	⚓	— Small beach left
			•2 / •3		— Highway bridge, preceded by Canyon Creek right
	50		•2		— Shallow drop between islands
	45		•2		
	40		•2		— Large islands with trees, Cornell Creek left
	35		•2		— Small beach left
	30		●2 / ●3 / •2	■	— **Wrap Rock,** stay left of large rock below
					— Large gravel bar right, shallow, stay left
	25		●2 / •2		— Bare bluff right
	20		●3		— **Gallop Drop,** big hole bottom right, Gallop Creek
			| •2		— Glacier Creek left
	15		●3	■	— **Landslide,** landslide area right
			•2		— Good playspot
	10		●3 / ●2 / ●3 / •2		— **Turtle Rock,** run left around huge boulder
	5	⬆ ⬆	●2 / ●3		— Camp shelters & house left
	12:00		●3	⛺	— **Fir Drop**
					— Douglas Fir Campground

RM 55

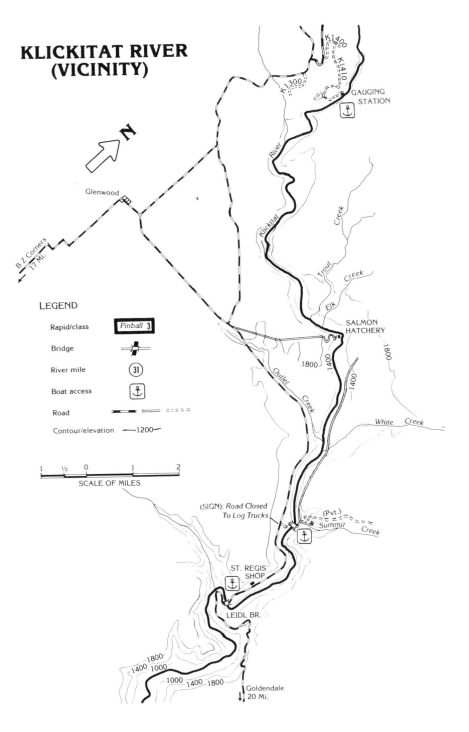

KLICKITAT RIVER (VICINITY)

N

Glenwood

B Z Corners
17 Mi.

K 1400
K 1410
K 1300

GAUGING
STATION

River

Klickitat

Creek

Troul

Creek

Elk

Creek

SALMON
HATCHERY

1800

1400

1800

1400

Outlet

Creek

White

Creek

(SIGN): *Road Closed
To Log Trucks*

(Pvt.)

Summit

Creek

ST. REGIS
SHOP

LEIDL BR.

1400 1800
1000

1000 1400 1800

Goldendale
20 Mi.

LEGEND

Rapid/class	Pinball 3
Bridge	
River mile	(31)
Boat access	⚓
Road	
Contour/elevation	—1200—

1   ½   0   1   2
SCALE OF MILES

10

Klickitat

Logged at - 3,400 cfs Pitt gauge (May)
Recommended water level - 1,700 to 3,500 cfs
Best time - Late April to late June
Rating - Advanced
Water level information - NOAA Tape (206) 526-8530
NOAA Information (206) 526-6087
River mile - 50.2 to 32.0; 18.2 miles
Time - 2 hours, 40 minutes; 6.8 mph
Elevation - 1705' to 860'; 46' per mile

Gauging Station to Leidl Bridge

The Klickitat flows through a narrow canyon cut 400 to 800 feet into a pine-forested plateau in eastern Washington. The geography is dramatically revealed by a short side trip to "viewpoint" between Leidl and Glenwood. The river scenery is punctuated by beautiful 200-foot high headwalls of columnar basalt. Because the Klickitat is so far east, it has the hot, dry climate of eastern Washington in May and June when the water levels are good. The surroundings are almost completely natural until you reach the fish hatchery, and even below this there are few signs of civilization.

Through the Columbia Gorge National Scenic Area Bill, Congress ordered the Forest Service to study the Klickitat above the mouth of the Little Klickitat for Wild & Scenic River designation. This is one of the most outstanding rivers in eastern Washington and richly deserves this protection. To help, write and urge the Forest Service to recommend Wild & Scenic designation for the Klickitat. Write to:

Art Dufault
Columbia Gorge National Scenic Area
902 Wasco Avenue
Hood River, OR 97031.

There are many spectacular basalt cliffs along the Klickitat. (Jeanne Martin photo)

Getting There

From BZ Corner on State Route 141, follow the county road across the White Salmon, about 20 miles to Glenwood. From there, it is a short drive either the put-in or the take-out at Leidl Bridge. Glenwood can also be reached by turning off State Route 142 about 11 miles west of Goldendale and driving about 30 miles on the county road to Glenwood.

Put-ins and Take-outs

The put-in is reached on a number of roads best explained by the vicinity map. You can make the turnoff just east of Glenwood or 3.5

miles east, just 100 yards west of the road that turns off to the fish hatchery (labeled with a sign). The road is largely paved, although there are some gravel stretches. You go about 6.5 miles until a turnoff is made on the dirt road labeled K1400, approximately 0.5 mile after the road labeled K1300. Three-fourths of a mile down K1400 an intersection is reached, at which point you should bear right on K1410. About 1.5 miles later, bearing left will take you 0.5 mile to an old gauging station at the river. The last 100 yards of the road are in bad condition. The equipment could be carried for this stretch.

There is a very good take-out or put-in about 100 yards below the Summit Creek bridge on the right. It is reached by turning off on a dirt road about 2.75 miles north of the St. Regis buildings above Leidl. A sign at the entrance to the road says "Road Closed to Log Trucks." A short, but steep, descent brings you to an intersection with a paved road used by the logging trucks. Turn left and in 100 yards the boat access site is on the right.

The take-out is on a good boat ramp at Leidl Campground. This is a Department of Wildlife site, requiring a license (see Introduction).

Water Level

The gauging station at the put-in is abandoned. Readings must be taken from the gauge at Pitt, which is many miles below the portion of the river covered by this log. Numerous tributaries enter the river below the logged run but above the gauging station. Since these tributaries are largely rain-fed, they constitute a greater percentage of the water on the Pitt gauge early in the season than they do later. The approximate percentages of water on the Pitt gauge that are present in the logged portion of the river are: January-March 32%, April 50%, May 70%, June and July 75%, August 65%, September-November 58% and December 43%. For normal running times, this produces recommended minimum and maximum discharge levels as follows:

	April	May	June	July	Aug
minimum	2,400	1,700	1,600	1,600	1,900
maximum	4,800	3,500	3,200	3,200	3,800

The log and description in this chapter are of the river at the higher end of the recommended water level. At low levels, the trip is much less demanding, many of the rapids decline one class in difficulty and there are probably only half a dozen class 3 rapids remaining. The water clears up at low levels, however, and the trip is so beautiful that it is almost preferable then.

Klickitat
Pitt Gauge
Recommend 1,700 to 3,500 cfs

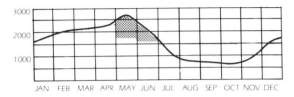

Special Hazards

The high gradient makes for nearly constant whitewater in the upper portion of the run. A bailer is essential for every raft that isn't self-bailing. At **higher water levels,** this section should be run only by very experienced boaters, as the lack of eddies could make for a very long swim in the event of an upset.

The water is melted snow and ice and very cold. It is always somewhat turbid due to glacial flour and becomes brown at the height of the spring runoff.

Logs are a great danger on the Klickitat. In some years, **logjams** have completely blocked the river channel.

The **dam** at the fish hatchery should be scouted on the left. It can be run on the left, but many boaters may wish to line it because of the ever-present debris.

Scenery

This is by far the most beautiful run in eastern Washington. There are no signs of civilization as the boat drifts through fragrant semi-open pine forests and many spectacular basalt cliffs.

The river below the Summit Creek bridge is very beautiful and swift, with few eddies, but little whitewater. There is a good boat ramp take-out at Leidl Campground. The river canyon from Leidl down to Wahkiacus is very pretty and remote, the only road access being on St. Regis logging roads from which the public is excluded. The river channel is often braided, however, and many logs clog it in places. There is class 1 water except for a nice class 2 drop just above Wahkiacus.

Camping

There is a lovely campsite at the put-in. There are also many beautiful semi-open meadows dotted with pine trees in the upper section which invite an overnight trip. An overnight trip is desirable at lower flows when boating time could approach four hours. Overnight camping is also attractive because of the few signs of civilization visible from the river.

Rapids

You will face continuous class 3 water from log time 0:35 to 0:51. This section is very demanding. The river surges and rolls over rocks and races between headwalls. There are almost no eddies. Past the fish hatchery, the difficulty eases, but the river is still very lively to Summit Creek bridge.

The Klickitat has cut deeply into the surrounding plateau

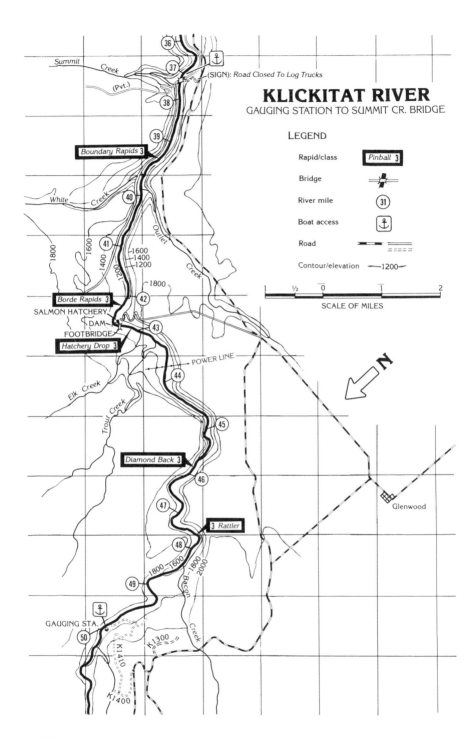

KLICKITAT RIVER
GAUGING STATION TO SUMMIT CR. BRIDGE

Summit Creek

(SIGN): *Road Closed To Log Trucks*

(Pvt.)

Boundary Rapids 3

White Creek

Outlet Creek

Borde Rapids 3

SALMON HATCHERY
DAM
FOOTBRIDGE

Hatchery Drop 3

POWER LINE

Elk Creek

Trout Creek

Diamond Back 3

3 Rattler

Bacon Creek

GAUGING STA.

LEGEND

Rapid/class	Pinball 3
Bridge	
River mile	31
Boat access	
Road	
Contour/elevation	—1200—

SCALE OF MILES
1   ½   0   1   2

N

Glenwood

102

RIVER MILE	RIVER TIME	LEFT BANK	RAPIDS	RIGHT BANK	DESCRIPTION
	2:00				
	55				— Scenic cliffs left
	50				— Put-in or take-out
					— Summit Creek Bridge
	45		●2 ●2		
	40		●2		
	35		●3 ●3		— Larger conglomerate rock
					— Conglomerate rock
					Boundary Rapids
	30		●2 ●2		
			●2		— White Creek left, big waves in class 2
RM 40	25		●2		— Outlet Creek right
					— Wonder Falls, created by large spring
	20		●2		
	15		●2		
	10		●2		
	5		●3 ●3		**Borde Rapids,** water into river from pipe right
					— Dam, scout left, either run or line left
					— Footbridge, state Salmon Hatchery right
	1:00		●3		**Hatchery Drop**
	55		●2		— Trout Creek left
			●2 ●2		— Cable
	50		●3 ●2 ●3		
	45		●3 ●3 ●2		
RM 45	40		●3 ●3		— Cliffs left
	35		●2 ●2 ●2		**Diamond Back**
	30		●2 ●2		— Small falls left — Deer Creek
					— Headwall left
	25		●2 ●2		— Small falls right — Skunk Creek
	20		●2 ●3 ●2		— Rock wall followed by headwalls left, then right
					Rattler, rock wall right
	15		●2		
	10		●2 ●2 ●2		— Rock wall left
	5				— Parrot Crossing
RM 50	12:00		●2 ●2		— Cable car and gauging station

At high water, class 3 rapids are nearly constant for two miles. (Jeanne Martin photo)

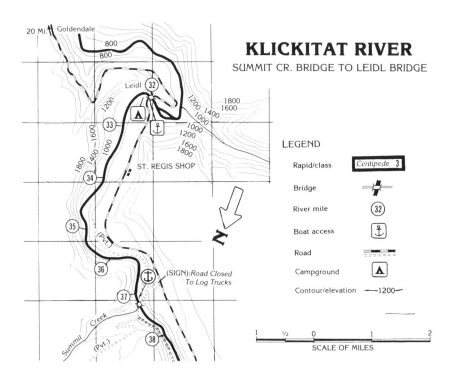

KLICKITAT RIVER

SUMMIT CR. BRIDGE TO LEIDL BRIDGE

LEGEND

Rapid/class	Centipede 3
Bridge	
River mile	32
Boat access	
Road	
Campground	
Contour/elevation	—1200—

SCALE OF MILES

RIVER MILE	RIVER TIME	LEFT BANK	RAPIDS	RIGHT BANK	DESCRIPTION
	4:00				
	55				
	50				
	45				
	40				
	35				
	30				
	25				
	20				
	15				
	10				
	5				
	3:00				
	55				
	50				
	45				— Boat ramp right
	40				— Leidl Bridge
	35		•2 •2		— Leidl Campground
	30				
	25		•2		
	20				
	15				
35	10				— Spectacular headwalls, first right, then left
	5		•2 •2		
	2:00		•2		— Headwall left

11

White Salmon

Logged at - 1,300 cfs Underwood gauge
Recommended water level - 700 to 1,300 cfs
Best time - June through August
Rating - Advanced
Water level information - NOAA Tape (206) 526-8530
NOAA Information (206) 526-6087
River mile - 12.3 to 5.0; 7.3 miles
Time - 1 hour, 37 minutes; 4.5 mph
Elevation - 630' to 300'; 45' per mile

BZ Corner to Northwestern Lake

The White Salmon flows off the south side of Mt. Adams on the eastern side of the Cascade mountains and runs about 35 miles south to the Columbia River. Mt. Adams glacial water is joined by water from numerous springs so that you can run the river throughout most of the summer. The numerous springs also promote lush vegetation along the banks, including maidenhair ferns and flowering plants. The White Salmon offers you the unique opportunity to enjoy simultaneously the beauty of near rain forest vegetation and the generally drier weather east of the crest of the mountains.

There is no such thing as a "white salmon," but many salmon take on a whitish cast when they head upriver to spawn. The great number of spawning salmon seen at the mouth of the river led to its name.

The run covered by this log is from just above the bridge at BZ Corner to the headwaters of Northwestern Lake, formed by Pacific Power and Light's Condit Dam. In the early 1980s this section of river was threatened by a proposed hydroelectric project which would have diverted most of the flow of the river through a long pipe, discharging it into Northwestern Lake. Friends of the White Salmon fought the

The White Salmon flows in a narrow channel that is often bordered by rock walls. (Dave Welch photo)

106

The White Salmon is a great kayaking river. (Dave Welch photo)

project, and its permit expired in 1983. In 1986 this section of the river became a Scenic river under the federal Wild & Scenic Rivers Act as part of the Columbia Gorge National Scenic Area Bill. The same Bill authorized the Forest Service to study, for possible Wild & Scenic designation, the section of the river upstream of Gilmer Creek to Trout Lake Creek.

Getting There

The White Salmon is paralleled by State Route 141 and is just over an hour's drive east of Portland.

Put-ins and Take-outs

The put-in is just off State Route 141 two blocks north of the road that turns off to the bridge over the river at BZ Corner. You may want to walk out on the bridge (some 135 feet over the river) to get a look at the whitewater in the gorge below. The put-in is owned by Jack Gross, and he has marked it with a sign by the highway that reads "White Salmon River Launch Point." He has provided a trail down to the river and a cable system for lowering rafts down to the river. In 1987 he charged $9.00 per private raft, $3.00 per person on commercial raft trips and $1.50 per kayaker. There is always someone there to help with launching, but Jack asks that you call ahead if you have a group larger than 25 people launching on a weekday. His phone number is (509) 493-3691.

The take-out is on a privately owned boat ramp at the head of

Northwestern Lake. There is a charge of $2.00 per raft and $1.00 per kayak to take out. To get to the boat ramp, turn off State Route 141 about 5 miles from the town of White Salmon or 2 miles from Husum on a paved road marked by signs to Northwestern Lake and Buck Creek Trail. Just beyond the bridge over the river, a left turn will lead you to the boat ramp and park.

Water Level

Because the White Salmon canyon is so narrow, water level is critical. A change of 300 cfs makes a big difference in the power of the river. I recommend between 700 and 1,300 cfs for a first trip. Above

For "Husum Days" (the weekend following the 4th of July weekend) there is a slalom race on the White Salmon. (Dave Welch photo)

1,500 cfs many of the rapids become one class higher, peppering this trip with class 4 rapids in Grasshopper, Corkscrew Falls, Water Spout and Stairstep Falls. Several of these are around blind corners in the canyon and are impossible to scout at higher water levels.

White Salmon
Underwood Gauge
Recommend 700 to 1,300 cfs

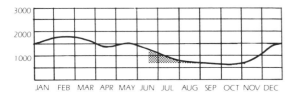

Special Hazards

Two-thirds of the way down the river is the town of Husum, where you should stop and look at **Husum falls,** an 8-foot drop at the bridge which is run by many kayakers but not often run by rafters. Kayakers submarine and rafters go nose-down and are likely to flip end over end. The land around the falls is owned by Phil Zoller and is open to those who wish to portage or line their boats around the falls.

The bridges over the river give you an opportunity to take "aerial" photos.
(Dave Welch photo)

Scenery

The upper part of this trip is in a spectacular, narrow canyon. The river is close to the highway, but due to the steep rock walls, varying from 50 to 100 feet high, it is isolated from the farms and road. In the last mile before reaching Husum, the river slope diminishes and you come out of the canyon into farm areas. You can get out on the right bank as soon as Husum bridge is sighted, in order to avoid running the falls, or you can line the falls on the left. Below Husum falls, there are lively rapids for the first mile and then more quiet drifting through beautiful forest, with much evidence of beavers, to Northwestern Lake.

Camping

Camping is available for a fee at Northwestern Lake. Otherwise, you must go west to Gifford Pinchot National Forest or east to the Horsethief Lake recreation area near the Dalles Dam.

Rapids

The trip begins with a bang in **Maytag Drop.** This class 4 involves some manuevering and a substantial drop into a hole at the end. Less aggressive boaters may want to portage or line it.

Between Maytag and **Husum Falls** there are several class 3 rapids. Four of these are larger than the others and have been named: Grasshopper, Corkscrew Falls, Water Spout and Stairstep. The average river slope is about 50 feet per mile, making the river velocity high. The river should be exciting for boaters with class 3 ability.

Grasshopper is fairly straightforward and can be read from the boat. **Corkscrew Falls** is the most difficult rapid at low water — stay well right to avoid the rocks and holes.

Waterspout is probably the most difficult rapid at high water because of the enormous spout created by large water flows. At high water, small rafts are well advised to carry a fair amount of water into Waterspout to avoid being thrown over by the force of the hydraulics.

Stairstep Falls consists of four drops. The first two and the last are good-sized while the third is more moderate. Run the first drop right of center and then pull left for the second drop. The third and fourth drops are straightforward.

The White Salmon is a cold river with its Mt. Adams glacial and spring water origins. The deep canyon also tends to screen out sun. Cold-water gear is nearly always necessary.

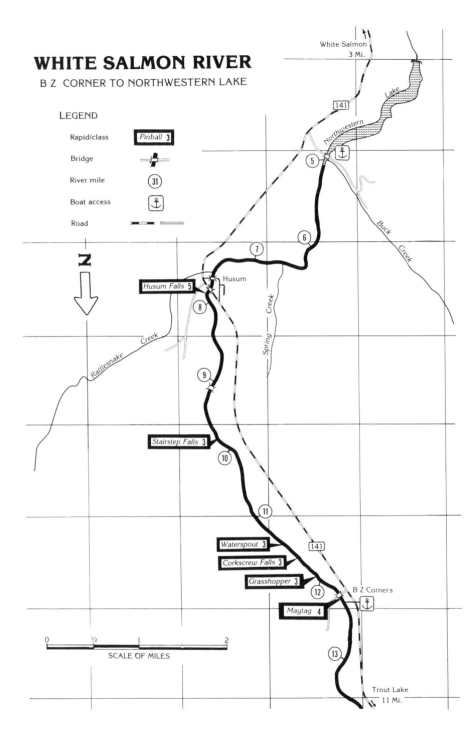

WHITE SALMON RIVER

B Z CORNER TO NORTHWESTERN LAKE

LEGEND

Rapid/class   Pinball 3

Bridge

River mile   31

Boat access

Road

N

White Salmon
3 Mi.

141

Lake

Northwestern

5

Buck Creek

6

7

Husum

Husum Falls 5

8

Spring Creek

Rattlesnake Creek

9

Stairstep Falls 3

10

11

141

Waterspout 3

Corkscrew Falls 3

Grasshopper 3

12

B Z Corners

Maytag 4

13

Trout Lake
11 Mi.

0   ½   1   2
SCALE OF MILES

112

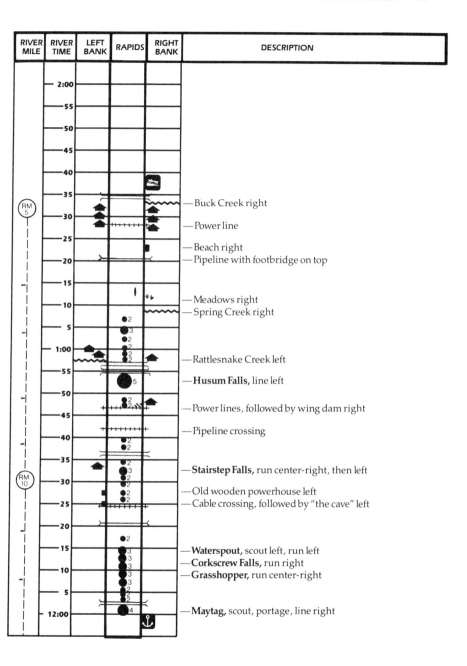

RIVER MILE	RIVER TIME	LEFT BANK	RAPIDS	RIGHT BANK	DESCRIPTION
	2:00				
	55				
	50				
	45				
	40				
	35				
RM 5	30				—Buck Creek right
	25				—Power line
	20				—Beach right
					—Pipeline with footbridge on top
	15				
	10				—Meadows right
	5		•2		—Spring Creek right
			3		
			•2		
	1:00		2		
			2		—Rattlesnake Creek left
	55		2		
			5		—**Husum Falls,** line left
	50		•2		
			2 2		—Power lines, followed by wing dam right
	45				
	40				—Pipeline crossing
			•2		
	35		•2		
			2		—**Stairstep Falls,** run center-right, then left
RM 10	30		3 2		
			•2		—Old wooden powerhouse left
	25		•2 2		—Cable crossing, followed by "the cave" left
	20				
	15		•2		
			3		—**Waterspout,** scout left, run left
	10		3 3 3		—**Corkscrew Falls,** run right
			3		—**Grasshopper,** run center-right
	5		2 2		
			2		
	12:00		4		—**Maytag,** scout, portage, line right

12

Middle Middle Fork Snoqualmie

Logged at - 1,500 cfs Middle Fork gauge
Recommended water level - 1,500 to 3,000 cfs
Best time - May and June
Rating - Advanced
Water level information - NOAA Tape (206) 526-8530
NOAA Information (206) 526-6087
King County (206) 255-2531
River mile - 57.1 to 49.5; 7.6 miles
Time - 2 hours, 2 minutes; 3.7 mph
Elevation - 850' to 530'; 42' per mile

Concrete Bridge to Tanner

Although the Middle Fork of the Snoqualmie is only 30 miles from Seattle and close to the town of North Bend, it seems remote. The river, fed by runoff from the snowfields on the west side of the Cascades, flows through a heavily forested area, and few man-made structures are visible through the trees. You'll encounter a wide variety of rapids as the water winds past the numerous granite boulders in its path. There are drops, narrow chutes, islands and deep pools, as well as the swirls around the boulders. In the lower stretch, difficult rapids are closely spaced and the boating is challenging.

This log covers a run known as the Middle Middle. Chapter 3 covers the upper Middle and the two can be combined for an overnight trip. You can also run the four-mile stretch from the take-out of this run down to the bridge at North Bend. It's known as the Club Stretch and has class 1 and 2 water and much visible development. The Middle Fork of the Snoqualmie is on the Nationwide Rivers Inventory as a potential Wild & Scenic River.

Getting There

To reach the Middle Middle, take exit 34 (Edgewick Road) from I-90 and drive north about 200 yards to Ken's Truck Stop. Since Ken's is near the take-out, most groups will want to drop off a car at the take-out before going on upriver.

Put-ins and Take-outs

You can get to the take-out by taking a left just before Ken's and driving 1.5 miles west on the road that parallels I-90. Turn right just past a lumber mill onto S. E. Tanner Road. You can see the river from the turnoff. Go 0.5 mile on S. E. Tanner and you'll find the take-out at the end of a 100-yard-long dirt road on the left, just below some power lines. There is room to park three or four cars in a gravel area along S. E. Tanner at the beginning of the dirt road.

To get to the put-in, drive north from Ken's approximately 200 yards and take a right at the T intersection. In about 0.9 mile, the road divides and then joins in another 1.2 miles.

Just after the two branches of the road rejoin, the pavement ends.

The Middle Fork has many chutes dropping into pools

Continue on the gravel road over the concrete bridge spanning the river. About 0.25 mile past the bridge, you'll cross a culvert, and about 200 yards past the culvert, you should turn right onto a poor dirt road. It's about 0.1 mile to the river. Although this put-in is on private land, it is open to the public.

You can also put in on a gravel bar on the left bank at log time 20 minutes. The bar is about 25 feet below the road, and you'll be able to see it through the trees as you drive in. To reach it, continue past the point where you can see the gravel bar until you come to a sharp left bend in the road. About 0.1 mile beyond the bend, turn off onto the very poor dirt road and take it to the put-in.

It's also possible to put in or take out at Mine Creek Campground, either to reach or avoid the significantly more difficult whitewater below the campground.

Water Level

You'll need a water level of 1,500 cfs to run the Middle Middle in a raft without scraping a lot of rocks. Kayaks will find good playspots at levels over 1,100 cfs. At water levels over 2,500 cfs there's much less danger of scraping on rocks, but the hydraulics become quite powerful because the drop is so great. Be very careful if you're boating the section at over 4,000 cfs, as the holes become very large. I compiled this log at 1,500 cfs when the water was quite technical and rocky but still very enjoyable. The river generally flows above 1,500 cfs only in May and June during the spring runoff.

For first trips, I recommend a level of less than 3,000 cfs; above that level, many of the rapids merge and the hydraulics are too powerful to be run safely by a boater who's not familiar with the section.

Middle Middle Fork Snoqualmie
Middle Middle Fork Gauge
Recommend 1,500 to 3,000 cfs

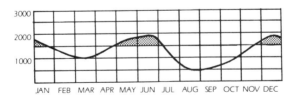

Special Hazards

None.

At lower water levels, many of the rapids are very rocky

Scenery

Forested banks drop to a boulder-strewn channel. The scenery's beautiful.

Camping

You can camp at Mine Creek Campground along the run and also at the Taylor River Campground about 9 miles farther up the Middle Fork Road.

Rapids

Since there are very few clear landmarks on the Middle Middle, you should be prepared to run difficult water at all times. Despite the unusual house-sized boulders in midchannel, you probably won't recognize **House Rocks Drop** until it's too late to scout. You'll probably want to run it starting left of center, directly toward the largest boulder (to avoid the large hole on the right top), then use a strong ferry to go right of the largest boulder.

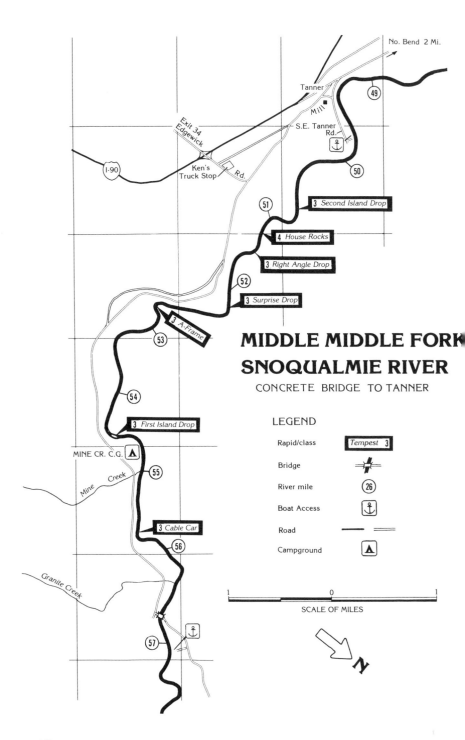

No. Bend 2 Mi.

Tanner

Mill

49

Exit 34
Edgewick

S.E. Tanner
Rd.

I-90

50

Ken's
Truck Stop

Rd.

51

3 Second Island Drop

4 House Rocks

3 Right Angle Drop

52

3 Surprise Drop

3 A-Frame

53

MIDDLE MIDDLE FORK
SNOQUALMIE RIVER

CONCRETE BRIDGE TO TANNER

54

3 First Island Drop

LEGEND

MINE CR. C.G.

Rapid/class	Tempest 3
Bridge	
River mile	26
Boat Access	
Road	
Campground	

55

Mine Creek

3 Cable Car

56

Granite Creek

1   0   1

SCALE OF MILES

57

N

RIVER MILE	RIVER TIME	LEFT BANK	RAPIDS	RIGHT BANK	DESCRIPTION
	2:00	⚓	2		—Power lines mark take-out
			2		—Good playspot at low water
RM 50	55	▲	2		
		▲	2		—Good playspot
	50		2		
	45			▲▲ 🏠	—Deck and houses right
	40		3 / 3	▬	—**Second Island Drop,** two class 3 rapids —High eroded dirt cliff right
	35	▲	3 / 3		—House in clearing left
	30		4		—**House Rocks Drop,** run left, then right
	25		3 / 3		—**Right Angle Drop**
	20		3 / 3		—Difficult class 3 —**Surprise Drop,** big hole at bottom, go left
	15		3		
	10		3		—Difficult class 3 at high water
	5	▲	3		—A-frame cabin left —**A-Frame Headwall Drop,** run left at bottom
	1:00		3 / 3		—Start right, go left, large keeper at end
	55		2		—Class 3 above 2500, big hole at bottom
	50		2	⚔	—Deep pool, logjam right
	45		2 / 2		—Difficult class 2, stay right
	40		3		—**First Island Drop,** run left of rock in middle of right channel, big drop at end
RM 55	35	⛺	3		—Easy class 3, Mine Creek Campground left
	30		2 / 2 / 3		
	25		2 / 3		—Easy class 3 —Cable Car —**Cable Car Rapids,** run right, good playspot
	20	⚓	2		—Gravel bar put-in
	15		1		
	10		1 / 1		
	5	〰			—Concrete bridge
	12:00			⚓	

13

Methow

Logged at -	7,200 cfs Pateros gauge
Recommended water level -	3,000 to 11,000 cfs
Best time -	May to mid-July
Rating -	Advanced
Water level information -	NOAA Tape (206) 526-8530
	NOAA Information (206) 526-6087
River mile -	27.2 to 1.4; 25.8 miles
Time -	3 hours, 48 minutes; 6.8 mph
Elevation -	1390' to 770'; 24' per mile

Carlton to Pateros

The Methow (pronounced Met' ow) originates high in the North
Cascades and runs with melting snow into the lake formed on the
Columbia River by Wells Dam. The Indian name for the river meant
"salmon falls river." It's a good description. The river has lots of
whitewater and fine runs of salmon. The valley through which it flows
is surrounded by dry, sagebrush-covered hills which look like the
setting for a Hollywood western. In fact, Owen Wister wrote *The
Virginian* while he was living in Winthrop, where the Chewuch joins
the Methow.

Most boating on the Methow takes place below the confluence of the
Chewuch and Methow at Winthrop. The run from Winthrop to
Carlton is mostly of class 1 difficulty but is punctuated by numerous
diversion dams and logjams. The diversion dams can have very
dangerous hydraulics and be life threatening; they should be portaged. The logjams rarely block the river completely, but they must be
avoided; two rafters were killed on this section of the river in 1983
when their raft was swept into a logjam.

This chapter focuses on the lower portion of the river from Carlton
to Pateros. At flows over 6,000 cfs, the Methow provides one of the best
"big water" trips in Washington, with few exposed rocks, but numerous big waves and holes. Since there is no federal land along this

There are good waves next to the cliff in Black Canyon

portion of the river, it is unlikely to become part of our federal Wild &
Scenic Rivers System, but it would make a fine addition to our state
scenic rivers system. The state program has no impact on private land
but could acquire more access and camping sites for fishermen and
boaters and provide a management plan to reduce conflicts between
local landowners and recreational users of the river.

Highway travelers can watch the action in Another Roadside Attraction

Getting There

The Methow is paralleled by State Route 153, which can be reached on State Route 20 (the North Cascades Highway) at Winthrop or on US 97 at Pateros.

Put-ins and Take-outs

The upper put-in is at the Department of Wildlife's fishing access at Carlton (conservation license needed — see Introduction). The access is just upstream of the bridge over the river at Carlton.

A put-in can also be made at log time 1 hour, 9 minutes from the Gold Creek Road. Turn off the highway about 7 miles north of the town of Methow on the Gold Creek Road and put in on your right about 200 yards up the road.

The most popular put-in for the big water in the lower part of the run is at the McFarland Creek fishing access (conservation license required). The fishing access is just above the bridge 3 miles upstream from the town of Methow. The trail down to the river is fairly steep.

The take-out near Pateros is along the north side of the highway at the upper end of the reservoir formed by Wells Dam. There is a large parking area along the old, abandoned highway here.

Water Level

As the Methow is snow-fed, it is a spring runoff river, generally only boatable from May through mid-July. A minimum flow of 3,000 cfs on the Pateros gauge is necessary to avoid scraping a raft on the rocks, but kayakers may enjoy the Methow down to about 2,000 cfs.

Methow
Pateros Gauge
Recommend 3,000 to 11,000 cfs

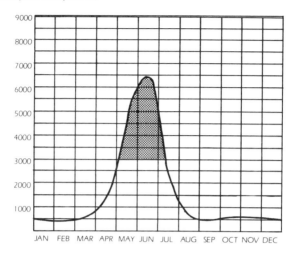

Dig into the holes!

The holes make great playspots (NW Outdoor Center photo)

Special Hazards

A maximum flow of 11,000 cfs on the Pateros gauge is recommended for a first trip. Above that level the water becomes very dirty, and there are very few eddies. The river often flows through trees along its bank. Above 9,000 cfs there is likely to be **driftwood** in the river. Many consider 9,000 cfs the ideal water level for fast boating on big water, but the water becomes much clearer below 7,500 cfs.

Scenery

Between Winthrop and Carlton there are many farms and ranches along the riverbank. The valley narrows at Carlton, and the orchards and alfalfa fields are fewer. Natural scenery becomes more prevalent, with pine-forested draws alternating with rock outcroppings.

Camping

Camping along the Methow is difficult. Almost all of the land along the river is privately owned. Permission should be obtained prior to pitching a tent. There are, however, several state and National Forest campgrounds within an easy commute of the river. Alta Lake State Park is only 2 miles off the main highway near Pateros. Campsites are about $4.00 per night and you should get there before the office closes at 8:00 PM. Foggy Dew Forest Service camp is about 7 miles up Gold Creek Road, which leaves the highway between Carlton and Methow.

Rapids

The lower section below Methow has many powerful class 3 rapids and one class 4 drop. Generally, experienced boaters can easily read the river and avoid large holes.

The **Black Canyon Rapids** are right where Black Canyon Creek joins the Methow. There is a substantial drop next to a sheer 100- to 150-foot river bluff. The drop starts after a sharp left bend and has a huge hole near the left side. The hole is known by an assortment of names, including Greyhound (so large it can swallow a bus) and Oarlock. However, the tag the Black Hole seems to have stuck. At most water levels there is a second, almost equally fearsome, hole somewhat downriver to the right. The best run is usually starting right center; when abreast of the Black Hole, move left and thread between the holes, running the large waves along the cliff on the left bank. Generally, it is better to err on the side of being too far right rather than too far left.

At log time 3:00, you'll reach an island with nearly equal flow around both sides. The right channel contains a huge hole that can be avoided but is tricky. The best approach is to take the left channel around the island.

A large rock formation is on the inside of a right bend at log time 3:19, forming the **Meteorite** (or the Lizard, Crocodile). It forms a hole over 9,000 cfs and is an obstacle at lower water levels.

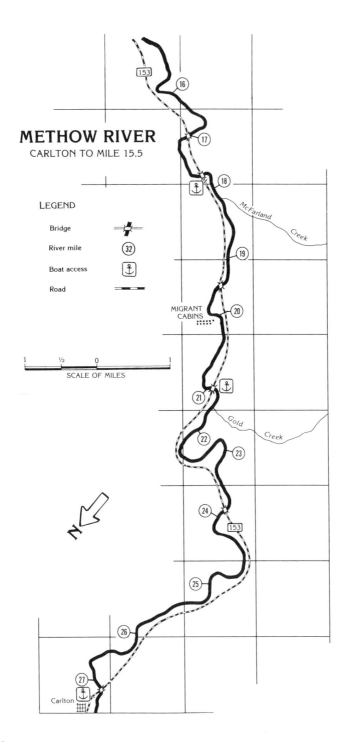

METHOW RIVER
CARLTON TO MILE 15.5

LEGEND

Bridge

River mile   (32)

Boat access

Road

SCALE OF MILES

½   0   1

MIGRANT CABINS

McFarland Creek

Gold Creek

153

16

17

18

19

20

21

22

23

24

153

25

26

27

Carlton

N

RIVER MILE	RIVER TIME	LEFT BANK	RAPIDS	RIGHT BANK	DESCRIPTION
	2:00		●2		—Rocky drop with headwall at end
	55		●2		
	50				
					—Highway bridge
	45		●2		
					—Highway bridge
	40	⚓	●2		—McFarland fishing access
	35		●2		
			●2		
	30		●1		
			●1		
	25		●1		—Highway bridge
	20				—Migrant Cabins left
RM 20			●1		
	15		●2		
			●1		
	10			⚓	—Highway bridge
			●1		—Gold Creek
	5		●2		
			●2		
	1:00		●1		
			●1		
	55				
	50		●1		
	45				—Highway bridge
	40				
	35		●1		
			●1		
	30				
RM 25	25				
	20			▲	—Power line by mansion
			●1		
	15		●1		
	10			▦	—Attractive home, left
			●1		
	5	▲			
	12:00	⚓			—Carlton bridge

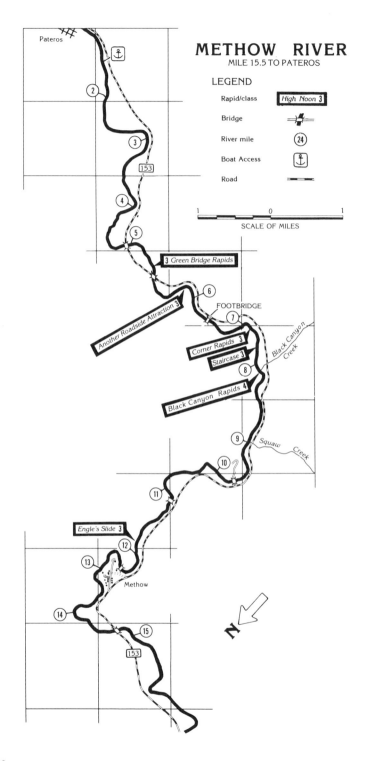

METHOW RIVER
MILE 15.5 TO PATEROS

LEGEND

Rapid/class	High Noon 3
Bridge	
River mile	24
Boat Access	⚓
Road	

SCALE OF MILES

Pateros

153

3 Green Bridge Rapids

FOOTBRIDGE

Another Roadside Attraction 3

Corner Rapids 3

Staircase 3

Black Canyon Creek

Black Canyon Rapids 4

Squaw Creek

Engle's Slide 3

Methow

153

N

RIVER MILE	RIVER TIME	LEFT BANK	RAPIDS	RIGHT BANK	DESCRIPTION
	4:00				
	55				
	50				
	45			⚓	— Take-out right bank near highway, take small channel, extreme right
	40				
	35		●2		
			●2		
	30		•1 ●2		
			●2		— Large hole left near concrete piling at under 6,000 cfs
	25		•1		
			●2	◄	
	20		●2		
			*		— Meteorite (Lizard, Crocodile)
RM 5	15				
	10		●3		— **Green Bridge Rapids**
					— Green Bridge
	5		●3		— **Another Roadside Attraction**
					— Large hole right
	3:00		❘*		— **Corner rapids**
	55		●3		— **Staircase** (Paddle Chase)
			●3		
	50		●4	～～～	— **Black Canyon Rapid** (Oarlock), scout right, sheer rock wall left, Black Canyon Creek immediately right
	45		•1		— White Bridge — one lane
	40		●2		
			●3		
	35		●3		
	30		●3		— **Engle's Slide,** two large holes
	25		*		— Hole under footbridge, right side
	20		●2		— Dilapidated footbridge
	15				— Town of Methow, out of sight, right bank
	10		●2		
RM 15	5		●2		
	2:00				

14

Chewuch

Logged at -	6,000 cfs Pateros gauge
Recommended water level -	5,000 to 10,000 cfs
Best time -	Late May and June
Rating -	Expert
Water level information -	NOAA Tape (206) 526-8530
	NOAA Information (206) 526-6087
River mile -	20.9 to 7.9; 13 miles
Time -	2 hours, 46 minutes; 4.7 mph
Elevation -	2390' to 1960'; 33' per mile

Camp Four to Five Mile Bridge

The Chewuch alternates between exciting rapid sections and quiet drifting. The rapids come in bunches near the mouths of the principal creeks feeding into the river. In between, you have ample opportunity to contemplate the clear water of the Chewuch framed by the red-brown bark of the ponderosa pines that line its banks. The forested Chewuch is a wonderful contrast with the sagebrush-dry Methow into which it empties.

Getting There

The Chewuch flows into the Methow River at Winthrop which is at the eastern end of the North Cascades Highway (State Route 20). On older maps the name of the river is spelled "Chewack." The spelling was recently changed to make the pronunciation more like that of the Indian word. The final "ch" is pronounced hard like a "k" so that the word sounds like "Chewuck."

Put-ins and Take-outs

The take-out is at the bridge 5 miles above Winthrop. There is a small eddy on the right hand side of the river just downstream from the bridge.

From the take-out, you should drive 0.2 mile up the Forest Service

Pine trees line the bank along Falls Creek Rapids

37 road on the east side of the river. Look down over the edge of the slope next to the river to inspect the irrigation dam, which you will have to run if you boat the last mile of the trip.

The main road, and the shuttle route, is the West Chewuch road, Forest Service 51 road. Up this road 0.75 mile from the bridge, you'll find a dirt road that turns off toward the river. It has no sign other than a number — 015. It leads to the site of the old Memorial Campground and provides a rough take-out point for those who wish to avoid the furious rapids between here and the bridge.

About 1.5 miles farther on the main road, you'll pass the entrance to the Eightmile Ranch (signed) on the right. A little over 2 miles farther, another potential put-in or take-out place is reached in the Methow Game Range (managed by the state Department of Wildlife). This is a large, open meadow area where it is easy to get a boat in or out of the river.

Just about 0.3 mile upstream, the West Chewuch road crosses Falls Creek and you reach Falls Creek Campground. Above the campground 0.5 mile is a dirt road that turns off toward the river, signed 082. At the upstream end of this road is the put-in spot at log time 1 hour, 9 minutes.

The uppermost put-in is at the Camp Four Campground, just downstream from the only bridge over the upper part of the river.

Water Level

The Chewuch is an exciting run from 5,000 to 10,000 cfs on the Pateros gauge. The Chewuch itself provides about 20 percent of the flow recorded on the Pateros gauge. Take a careful look at the last mile above the take-out before you run it at high levels; it has continuous, powerful rapids which develop huge holes at high water levels.

Chewuch
Pateros Gauge
Recommend 5,000 to 10,000 cfs

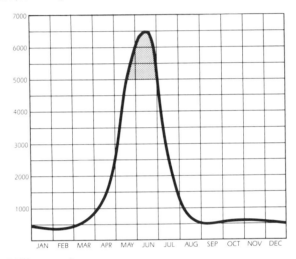

Special Hazards

Check the irrigation diversion **dam** at log time 2 hours, 43 minutes before you run the last mile of the trip. At most of the recommended water-level range, it can safely be run, but it might form a dangerous keeper at other levels. Low water levels reveal a piece of **metal** sticking up from the dam to the left of the center channel; stay to the right of center.

The Chewuch has many **logs** in it and is a small enough river that they chould easily block the channel. Check the rapid sections for blocking logs before you run the river, and stay alert!

Scenery

The Chewuch flows through a pretty valley covered with semi-open pine forest. The ponderosa pines along the banks of the river are beautiful. There is little evidence of human activity along the river above Eightmile Creek. The trip provides a contrast to the bigger, more developed Methow. The Okanogan National Forest has recommended the Chewuch for addition to our national Wild & Scenic Rivers system. If you would like to help get permanent protection for this outstanding river, contact the Northwest Rivers Council, listed in the Preface.

Camping

There are several campgrounds situated right along the Chewuch: Falls Creek, Chewuch and Camp Four. After mid-May, a fee is charged for the use of Falls Creek Campground.

Rapids

Twentymile Creek Rapids give you a taste of the Chewuch's excitement. There are several more sets of fast boulder and hole dodging, lasting from 200 yards to a mile. Check out **Boulder Creek Rapids,** the last mile of the trip, before you run it. It is continuous class 3 to 4 with no eddy large enough for a raft below the mouth of Boulder Creek. I like to think of it as "Mr. Toad's Wild Ride." There is an eddy on river left just below the mouth of Boulder Creek. You may want to stop here and secure your gear. Once a raft leaves this eddy, it is committed to going all the way to the take-out — there is no place to stop!

Falls Creek Campground allows you to camp right by the river

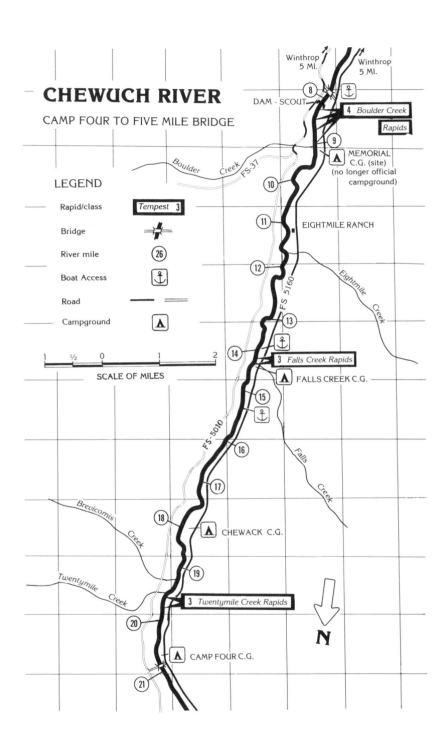

CHEWUCH RIVER

CAMP FOUR TO FIVE MILE BRIDGE

Winthrop 5 MI.

Winthrop 5 MI.

DAM - SCOUT

8

4 *Boulder Creek*

Rapids

9

MEMORIAL C.G. (site) (no longer official campground)

Boulder Creek FS-37

10

11

EIGHTMILE RANCH

LEGEND

Rapid/class	*Tempest* 3
Bridge	
River mile	26
Boat Access	
Road	
Campground	

12

FS 5160

Eightmile Creek

13

14

3 *Falls Creek Rapids*

FALLS CREEK C.G.

15

FS-5010

16

Falls Creek

1 ½ 0 1 2

SCALE OF MILES

17

18

Brevicornis Creek

CHEWACK C.G.

19

Twentymile Creek

3 *Twentymile Creek Rapids*

20

N

CAMP FOUR C.G.

21

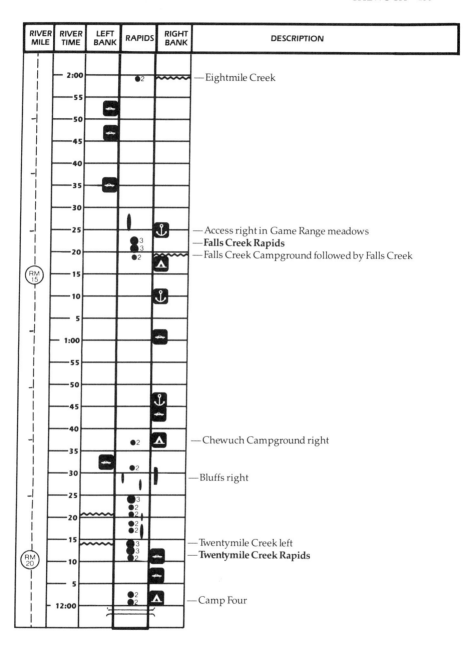

RIVER MILE	RIVER TIME	LEFT BANK	RAPIDS	RIGHT BANK	DESCRIPTION
	2:00		●2		—Eightmile Creek
	55				
	50				
	45				
	40				
	35				
	30				
	25				—Access right in Game Range meadows
	20		●3 ●3		—**Falls Creek Rapids**
			●2		—Falls Creek Campground followed by Falls Creek
RM 15	15				
	10				
	5				
	1:00				
	55				
	50				
	45				
	40				
	35		●2		—Chewuch Campground right
	30		●2		—Bluffs right
	25		●3		
	20		●2 ●2		
			●2 ●2		
	15				—Twentymile Creek left
RM 20			●3 ●3		—**Twentymile Creek Rapids**
	10		●2		
	5				
	12:00		●2 ●2		—Camp Four

A rock wall on the right bank marks the entrance into Boulder Creek Rapids

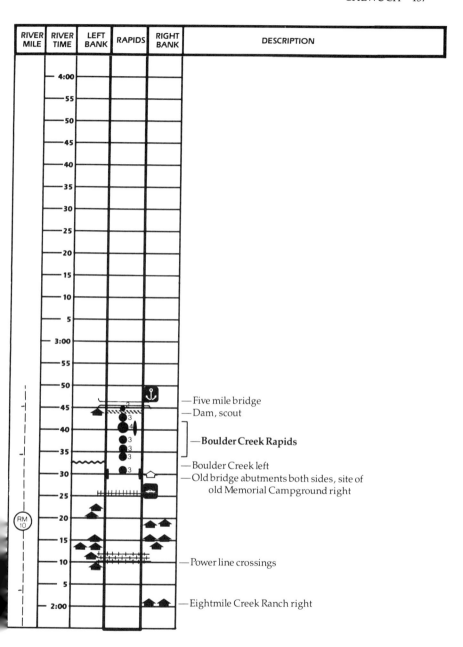

RIVER MILE	RIVER TIME	LEFT BANK	RAPIDS	RIGHT BANK	DESCRIPTION
	4:00				
	55				
	50				
	45				
	40				
	35				
	30				
	25				
	20				
	15				
	10				
	5				
	3:00				
	55				
	50				—Five mile bridge
	45		2		—Dam, scout
	40		3, 4		
	35		3, 3, 3		**—Boulder Creek Rapids**
	30		3		—Boulder Creek left
	25				—Old bridge abutments both sides, site of old Memorial Campground right
RM 10	20				
	15				
	10				—Power line crossings
	5				
	2:00				—Eightmile Creek Ranch right

15

Middle Sauk

Logged at - 6,900 cfs Sauk gauge
Recommended water level - 4,000 to 10,000 cfs
Best time - Late April to late July
Rating - Expert
Water level information - NOAA Tape (206) 526-8530
NOAA Information (206) 526-6087
River mile - 31.7 to 21.4; 10.3 miles
Time - 2 hours, 4 minutes; 5.0 mph
Elevation - 900' to 502'; 39' per mile

White Chuck to Darrington

The Sauk derives its name from the Sah-kee-ma-hu band of the Skagit Indian tribe, which lived in the area. The Upper Sauk, above White Chuck, was covered in Chapter 4. The White Chuck adds significantly to the amount of water in the river, which allows this section to be run at lower readings on the Sauk gauge. The White Chuck also adds considerable glacial silt to the Sauk, turning it deep green.

Since most of the flow of the Sauk comes from melting snow and ice, it is very cold. Wetsuits are strongly advised even when the weather is warm. Helmets are also advisable as the Sauk is rocky. Anyone thrown from a raft may well hit his or her head on a rock. Commercial rafting companies require both wetsuits and helmets for all of their passengers.

At the recommended water levels, the Middle Sauk is one of the most exciting and scenic whitewater trips in Washington. It is protected as a scenic river under the federal Wild & Scenic Rivers Act and is one of the most challenging half-dozen raft runs in the state.

Getting There

The river is approached through Darrington, which is 65 miles northeast of Seattle on State Route 530.

138

Over the top and into a hole in Jaws

The Mountain Loop Highway provides access to the Sauk. It leaves the south side of Darrington near the river and eventually crosses the Sauk just above the mouth of the White Chuck River. To get to it, go one block east of the 90-degree turn in the main road in Darrington, turn right, and then, after several blocks, left at a "T" intersection and follow the signs to "Mountain Loop Highway, Granite Falls."

An alternative road (sometimes impassable) is a narrow, winding dirt road on the northeast side of the river. To reach it, take a right immediately after crossing the bridge over the river near Darrington.

Put-ins and Take-outs

The take-out is at an unimproved boat ramp just downstream from the west (Darrington) side of the bridge over the river near Darrington.

An alternative take-out for those who want a shorter trip is at Snohomish County's Bachman Park at log time 1 hour, 34 minutes. This take-out is not easy to see from the river and you should memorize some landmarks in advance. It's just a little downstream from the end of the large tree-covered island around the right side of which the river has cut a new channel (the best boating route).

The put-in is at the new boating access site just downstream from the mouth of the White Chuck River. To reach it, turn left off the Mountain Loop Highway about 200 yards after crossing the bridge over the Sauk.

Water Level

The recommended water level ranges from 4,000 cfs to 10,000 cfs on the Sauk gauge. To avoid scraping bottom, a large raft needs approximately 4,000 cfs. Kayaks and small inflatables may enjoy the river at lower levels, however.

Maximum recommendation is 10,000 cfs. Above 10,000 cfs the level of difficulty increases significantly. The river is likely to be carrying a number of logs which present a hazard in rapids. The river also carries more silt above 10,000 cfs, turning it gray and making river reading difficult, as whitewater does not stand out from the river. Holes are often only seen from some 20 to 25 feet away, requiring quick maneuvering. At higher levels, the water also flows more quickly, bringing you up on rocks and holes very rapidly.

At flows above 15,000 cfs, the rapids in the first 30 minutes of the trip should all be increased one level in difficulty. The stretch becomes class 4 to 5. There are NO eddies, NO opportunities to bail, NO time to rest, and LITTLE opportunity to rescue someone if necessary. This becomes a very dangerous stretch of water at higher flows.

The Sauk River gauge is located below the confluence of the Suiattle and the Sauk. The approximate percentage of the Sauk gauge reading which is actually present in the Middle Sauk varies by months as follows:

May	June	July	Aug	Sept
57%	52%	51%	41%	40%

Middle Sauk
Sauk Gauge
Recommend 4,000 to 10,000 cfs

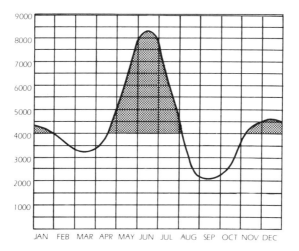

Special Hazards

You should be very careful to obtain the most recent gauge readings possible and to watch the weather. The Sauk is subject to **rapid fluctuations** in water level and can come up so fast after a rain or a period of hot weather that you can almost see it rise. Great caution must be exercised with regard to the water level. It could be at 8,000 cfs yesterday and 16,000 cfs today, making it a very dangerous run.

Scenery

The river flows through heavily forested banks between snow-covered mountains. The first two-thirds of the trip is quite remote. You're likely to see wildlife, particularly deer.

Camping

Camping is available at Bachman County Park — one of the possible take-outs — and at the Forest Service's Clear Creek Campground, just upriver from Bachman Park.

Rapids

The first few miles of the trip (up to log time 28 minutes) are very demanding. It is very difficult to scout any of the rapids on this section due to the twisting river channel, steep gradient and heavily forested banks. The rapids are choked with boulders and good river reading skills are essential. This section of the river is very dangerous at flows above those recommended in this book.

The **Alligator Drop** takes its name from a large, flat rock in the middle of the river. It forms a hole capable of flipping a raft at flows over 8,000 cfs.

Jaws (or Demon Seed) is the most difficult rapid on the river. It is well worth scouting, which can be done on the right side. Land above the island on the right (watch for a small portion of the river heading right, through boulders — this is the water going to the right of the island). Wade across the channel to the island and walk downriver to scout. There is a good trail in the middle of the island once you get below the logs piled at its head. Below the island is a large rock, known as Demon Seed.

The rapid is usually run down the left side of the island and around the right side of Demon Seed. Then you should ferry to the left of the rocks in the center below. For many years, there was a logjam on the right below Demon Seed at the location shown in the diagram. The logjam was washed away in 1987 but may return in future years. If it does, it is important to ferry well left, away from the logs.

Oar rafts and kayakers can often make the ferry to the left of Demon Seed, avoiding the need to make the strong ferry below it. For a raft, this largely depends upon your ability to avoid filling your boat with water in the numerous holes on the approach down the left side of the island.

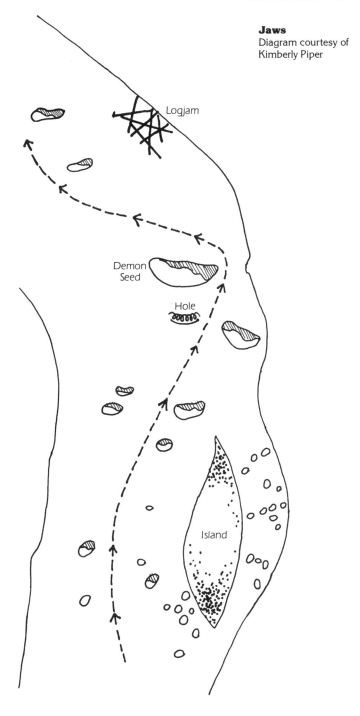

Jaws
Diagram courtesy of
Kimberly Piper

Logjam

Demon
Seed

Hole

Island

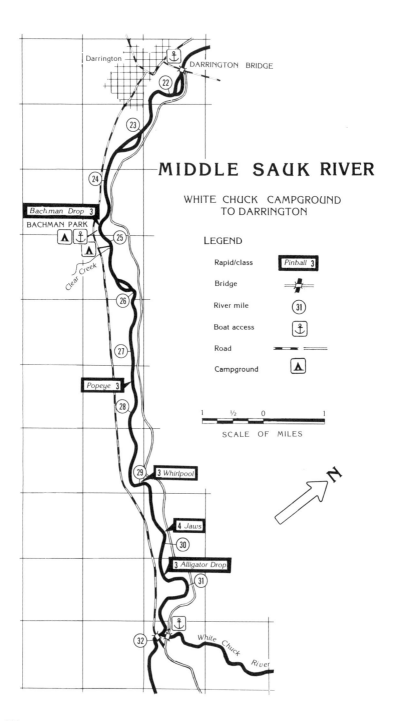

MIDDLE SAUK RIVER

WHITE CHUCK CAMPGROUND TO DARRINGTON

LEGEND

Rapid/class	Pinball 3
Bridge	
River mile	31
Boat access	
Road	
Campground	

SCALE OF MILES
1   ½   0   1

Darrington
DARRINGTON BRIDGE
22
23
24
Bachman Drop 3
BACHMAN PARK
Clear Creek
25
26
27
Popeye 3
28
29 3 Whirlpool
4 Jaws
30
3 Alligator Drop
31
32
White Chuck River

N

RIVER MILE	RIVER TIME	LEFT BANK	RAPIDS	RIGHT BANK	DESCRIPTION
	2:00				—Darrington Bridge
					—Small beach left
	55				—Gravel bar island left
					—Rip-rap left
	50				—Shed left
	45		•2		
			•2		—Dry channel to right of island
	40		•2		
	35		•3		—Bachman Park left, followed by **Bachman Drop**
	30		•3		—Channel left of island dry except at flood
RM 25	25		•2		—Clear Creek Campground left
			•2		—Clear Creek left
	20		•2		
			•2		
	15		•2		
			•2		
	10		•2 *		—Rock coming out from right bank
	5		* •2		—Large rock center channel
	1:00		•2		
	55		•2		
	50		•2		
			•3		**Popeye** (Lucifer's Hammer) big, fun waves
	45		•3		
	40		•2		
			•2		—Murphy Creek left
	35		•3		—**Whirlpool,** headwall-stay right at bottom
	30		•2		—Goodman Creek left
			•2		
	25		•3		
			•4		—**Jaws** (Demon Seed) scout right on island
	20		* •3		—Run right of mid-stream rock
			•3		
	15		•3		—**Alligator Drop**
			•2		
	10				—Road right, deepest channel far right
	5		•3		
			•2		
RM 30	12:00		•3		—White Chuck river right

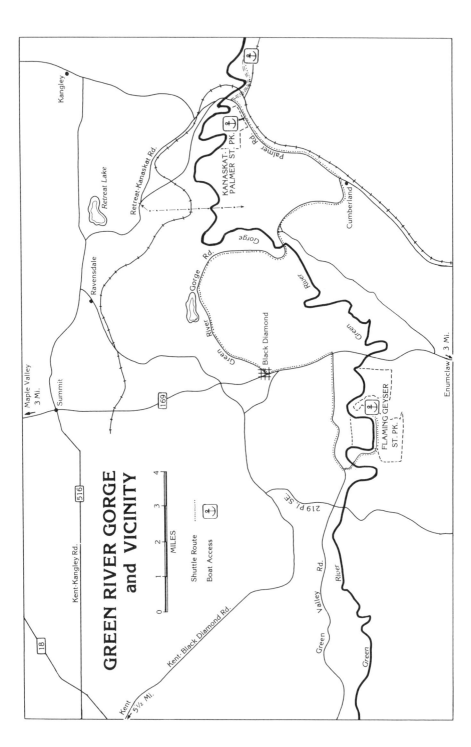

GREEN RIVER GORGE and VICINITY

MILES

0 1 2 3 4

Shuttle Route ....

Boat Access

Maple Valley 3 Mi.

Summit

516

18

Kent-Kangley Rd.

169

Kangley

Retreat Lake

Ravensdale

Retreat-Kanaskat Rd.

KANASKAT-PALMER ST. PK.

Palmer Rd.

Cumberland

Gorge

Green River

Gorge Rd.

Green River

Black Diamond

FLAMING GEYSER ST. PK.

Enumclaw 3 Mi.

219 Pl. SE

Green Valley Rd.

Green River

Green River

Kent-Black Diamond Rd.

Kent 5½ Mi.

146

16

Green

Logged at - 1,800 cfs Howard Hansen gauge
Recommended water level - 1,100 to 2,300 cfs
Best time - April and May
Rating - Expert
Water level information - NOAA Tape (206) 526-8530
NOAA Information (206) 526-6087
Corps of Engineers (206) 764-6702
River mile - 59 to 45.1; 13.9 miles
Time - 3 hours, 37 minutes; 3.8 mph
Elevation - 820' to 205'; 44' per mile

Palmer to Flaming Geyser Park

The Green River Gorge is one of the most beautiful river canyons in Washington State. The Green River has cut its way through a plateau approximately 30 miles southeast of Seattle. It descends from about 800 to 200 feet above sea level and then emerges into a broad valley. From this point it calmly flows north into Elliott Bay in Seattle.

This gorge has been proposed as a "Hanging Gardens" state park and the river is being considered for addition to our state scenic rivers system. There are numerous mines hereabouts, and the town of Black Diamond is named for the nearby coal deposits. In addition to coal, mercury has been found in this area. Flaming Geyser State Park (the take-out) acquired its name from a flame that still burns atop an abandoned gas well.

The river cannot be run much above Palmer, as it forms the Tacoma watershed, and access is restricted. The Army Corps of Engineers' Howard Hansen Dam is a few miles above the put-in and controls the flow of water through the gorge.

Getting There

Black Diamond, where most boaters meet to run the Gorge, is on State Route 169. State Route 169 can be reached by taking exit 4 from

147

There's a great playspot at Paradise Ledge. *(NW Outdoor Center photo)*

I-405 in Renton toward Enumclaw and Maple Valley or, from the south, by exiting I-5 on State Route 18 and going 11 miles until it intersects State Route 516, the Kent-Kangley road, which in turn intersects State Route 169 in 5 miles.

The Green River can then be reached on a number of small county roads which are shown on the vicinity map.

Put-ins and Take-outs

The uppermost put-in is reached on an unmarked gravel road that turns off Palmer Road just south of the river in Palmer. Cross a pair of railroad tracks and drive about 1.1 miles until you see a 20-foot section of dirt road on your left (toward the river) connecting with a dirt road paralleling the gravel one you are on. Turn down onto the dirt road and drive about 20 yards back toward Palmer. The put-in is below a clearing on your right. It is a steep carry down to the eddy.

Two put-ins are available in Kanaskat-Palmer State Park. Enter the park and bear left at the first intersection, then follow the boating signs (which look just like the light boat put-in and take-out symbols in this book) to the put-ins. The signs to the right will lead you to a parking lot. From here a wide 40-yard path leads through the bushes to the river and the "Dangerous River Conditions Ahead" sign just above Ledge Drop 1. The signs to the left lead to a parking area from which a longer and steeper path (best suited to kayakers) leads down to a large eddy just above Ledge Drop 2.

Light boats can also put in or take out at the Green River Gorge Resort, right by the Franklin Bridge. There is a $2.00 charge for using the steep (150 vertical feet) 300-yard trail down to the river.

The take-out is on the lawn of the picnic area at Flaming Geyser State Park. Follow the signs to the park from State Route 169. The picnic area is about 1.5 miles into the park.

Water Level

The most accurate gauge for judging river conditions in the gorge is the Howard Hansen gauge. Good levels for running are between 1,100 and 2,300 cfs. Good boaters, who are familiar with the gorge, will run it at higher levels, but many of the rapids increase a half class in ranking at those levels. If you are willing to make the tough carry to put in below Franklin Bridge at the resort, the lower gorge can be run at 900 cfs. Kayakers can scrape down the upper gorge on about 800 cfs and the lower gorge on about 600 cfs. A call to the Army Corps of Engineers office, at (206) 764-6702, puts you in touch with a regulator who can explain how much water will be released at various times for about the next 24 hours. The spillways on the dam are set Friday afternoon, and river flow remains constant all weekend unless there is sudden flooding.

Green
Howard Hansen Gauge
Recommend 1,100 to 2,300 cfs

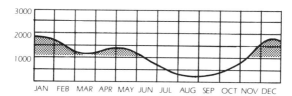

Special Hazards

Water is usually high enough to run the gorge only when the weather is **cold** or it is raining. Wetsuits are a must. Because the channel is very **rocky,** helmets are advisable for rafters. Kayakers should always wear helmets.

Scenery

The Green River Gorge is 150 to 300 feet deep and is protected under state law as a special conservation area. Almost 2 miles of Eocene sedimentary rocks and fossils are exposed, revealing layers of geological history.

Wolf Bauer in a *Seattle Times* article commented, "Down its cliffs and gentler draws remain untouched first-growth stands of evergreens, hiding moss and fern-covered grottos and myriads of tiny waterfalls seeping from the canyon walls. Freshness and moisture permeate the floor of the canyon in its shadowy twilight to nurture rain-forest type vegetation, water oriented birds, and man's awed senses within its massive cathedral-like halls. Placid pools like miniature chain lakes create an occasional corridor of silence into which only faint and muffled hints of rushing water may penetrate from around the bend— disturbed only by an occasional kingfisher, merganzer, water ouzel or trout rippling the water's impatient slack."

Camping

There are many good campsites at Kanaskat-Palmer State Park near the put-in. A fee is charged for camping at the park.

Rapids

The gorge can perhaps best be described as twisting and boulder choked. There are so many rocks in the channel that even expert paddlers and oarsmen will find it difficult not to scrape some rocks in many areas. As can be seen from the log, the main gorge stretch from river time 40 minutes to river time 2:00 is very demanding. Class 3 water is nearly constant, and you must be prepared to run it at all times. It is pointless to discuss scouting these rapids or which way to run many of them, as they are often upon you before you know it. This is a small, technical stream requiring very precise maneuvering to avoid destroying your craft, or yourself, on the rocks.

The upper section, above the outlet of the fish hatchery at river time 40 minutes is quite straightforward and could even be canoed by experts, with the possible exception of **Railroad Bridge Drop.** As you approach this drop, there is a definite horizon line. The river drops about 4 feet in 7 or 8 feet. The drop can usually be run just to the right of center, but there are several rocks and holes that could be dangerous to the unwary.

Ledge Drop 1 is just around the bend below the outlet from the fish hatchery. There is also a sign visible from the river at this point warning of dangerous river conditions. Again, you will see a horizon line from above, followed by boiling whitewater. The drop can be scouted by landing on the right side, just below the fish hatchery outlet. To scout, you must scramble over the hillside and down around the bend. The run is usually right down the center. You must pay attention, however, to the powerful hydraulics and numerous holes. Ledge Drop 1 is marginally a class 4 rapid at 1,800 cfs, but with 20 percent more water (still within recommended discharge ranges for the run) the hydraulics become very powerful.

You will encounter **Pipeline** (Ledge Drop 3) at a fairly sharp right bend in the river. A boulder bar extends out from the inside of the bend and considerable water works its way through it. There is enough water to boat only on the left or outside of the bend. After getting around the bend, work back toward the right, as a very large hole forms on the left. This large hole can have a breaking reversal that resembles the famous Pipeline Surf in Hawaii. The drop is a steep one, and much maneuvering is required to avoid the rocks and hit the reversal squarely at the bottom.

A high-tension power line crossing the canyon high overhead is the warning for **Mercury** and **The Nozzle.** These two class 4 rapids are quite difficult as they occur about 50 yards apart. "Screw up on

Shooting through The Nozzle

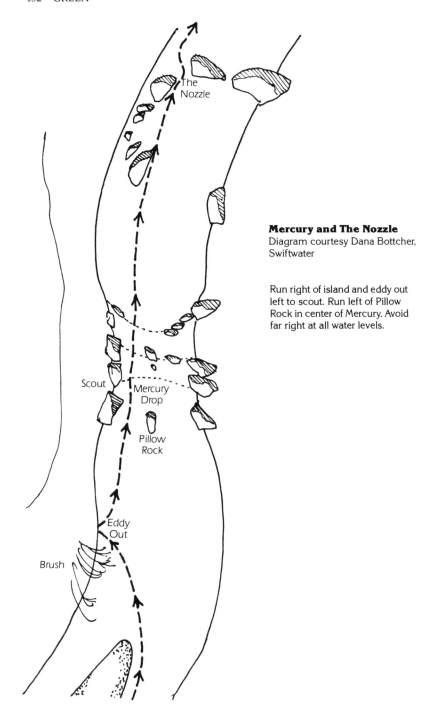

Mercury and The Nozzle
Diagram courtesy Dana Bottcher,
Swiftwater

Run right of island and eddy out
left to scout. Run left of Pillow
Rock in center of Mercury. Avoid
far right at all water levels.

Mercury and you'll get Nozzlized," say the old hands. Just below the power line there is a brush-covered boulder bar in the middle of the river. Take the right channel and, after rounding the end of the bar and a short (10 yards) class 3 rapid, pull into the left bank and scout Mercury and The Nozzle. Stay well left; if you're in the center of the channel, you'll never make it to the eddy. Scouting is not easy, as the bank is steep, rock strewn and brushy. However, even an expert river runner would have difficulty running these two rapids without first scouting them.

Usually the best run is to the right of the pillow rock at the center top of Mercury, then down just to the right of the large sloping rock forming the left side of The Nozzle.

The Nozzle is formed by three large rocks nearly choking off the flow of the river. Most of the water hits the upstream rock to the left and is deflected to the right where it slams into the middle rock and then squirts to the left between the two rocks through a gap only 10 to 12 feet wide. Some of the water passes through a passage too small to be boated to the right side of the middle rock. This flow of water around both sides of the middle rock threatens to broach or wrap your boat on the rock. A good run skirts the upstream side of the left-hand rock while paddling or rowing to slow your approach to the middle rock, and then quickly turning left as soon as you come abreast of the opening, to shoot through The Nozzle.

Below the Franklin Bridge near the Green River Resort, the difficulty eases, though kayakers should beware the "squirrely" water just below the bridge on the left. Shortly below the resort, you will reach **Paradise Ledge,** a great kayak playspot. A hotspring, caused by an underground fire in a coalmine, is on the left side at log time 2:18. It is marked by an old telephone pole set in a gully above it. The plastic that has been used to line a pool for the hot spring is also visible, and there is a good eddy to pull into. The hot spring is only about 70-75 degrees, but it can be very welcome on a cold day.

The difficulty of **Slide Drop** has eased greatly in the last few years because the river has cleared much of the channel. The rapid was created by rocks, trees and earth sliding into the river from the left side of the gorge. It can be scouted by landing on the left, just above the slide area. The best run of the drop is to the left of the pillow rock in the center. Although Slide Drop has become easier recently, remain alert. The instability of the cliffs in this area could easily result in new slides. The drop should be approached with caution. In a recent year, a fallen tree extended all the way across the river, requiring either a hair-raising run under the log or a carry around.

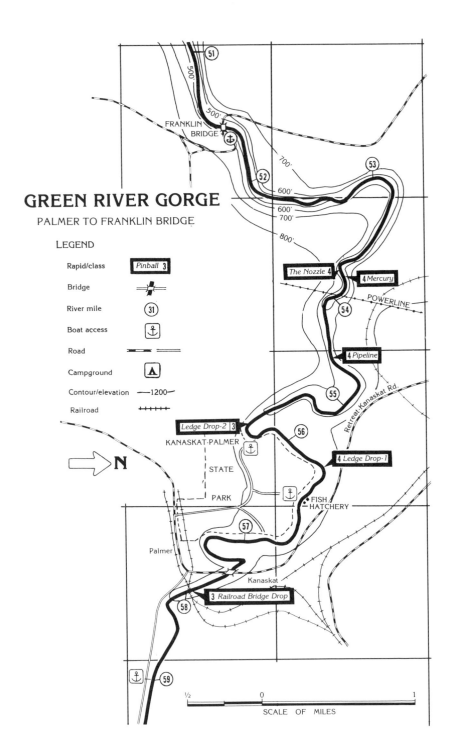

GREEN RIVER GORGE
PALMER TO FRANKLIN BRIDGE

LEGEND

Rapid/class	Pinball 3
Bridge	—✈—
River mile	③¹
Boat access	⚓
Road	━━ ═══
Campground	🅰
Contour/elevation	—1200—
Railroad	+++++

N

FRANKLIN BRIDGE

The Nozzle 4

4 Mercury

POWERLINE

4 Pipeline

Ledge Drop-2 3

KANASKAT-PALMER

STATE

PARK

4 Ledge Drop-1

Retreat-Kanaskat Rd.

FISH HATCHERY

Palmer

Kanaskat

3 Railroad Bridge Drop

½   0   1

SCALE OF MILES

RIVER MILE	RIVER TIME	LEFT BANK	RAPIDS	RIGHT BANK	DESCRIPTION
	2:00				—Franklin Bridge
			3		—Run left
	55		3		—Run right, then cut left through boulders between
			2		drops
	50		2 2		
			3		—Run right
	45		2 2		
			3		—Island, go left
			3		
	40		3		—Overhanging rock
			3		
	35		3		
			3		
	30		3		—Run right
			3		—Cabin high on right, hard class 3
	25		3		
			4		**The Nozzle,** scout left, run through slot
	20		4		**Mercury,** scout left, run left center
			2		—Power line
	15		2		
			2		
	10		3		
			4		**Pipeline,** run left then cut back right
	5		2		
			3		—Run just right of stump, far right channel has rock
RM 55	1:00		3		in center
			3		
	55		3		—Run far right
			3		—Exposed rock bluff left
	50		3		
			3		
	45		3		**Ledge Drop 2**
			3		—Tree high on rock on right
	40		4		
			2		**Ledge Drop 1,** scout right, run center, sign left
	35		2 3		"Dangerous River Conditions Ahead"
					—Technical, but weak, class 3, go right of rocks and
	30		2		trees forming island
			2		
	25		2		—Kanaskat-Palmer Sate Park, left
	20				—Kanaskat-Palmer Bridge
	15		3		**Railroad Bridge Drop,** run just right of center
					—Old railroad bridge
	10		2		—Old bridge abutment, right
			2 2		
	5				—Large island, left
	12:00				

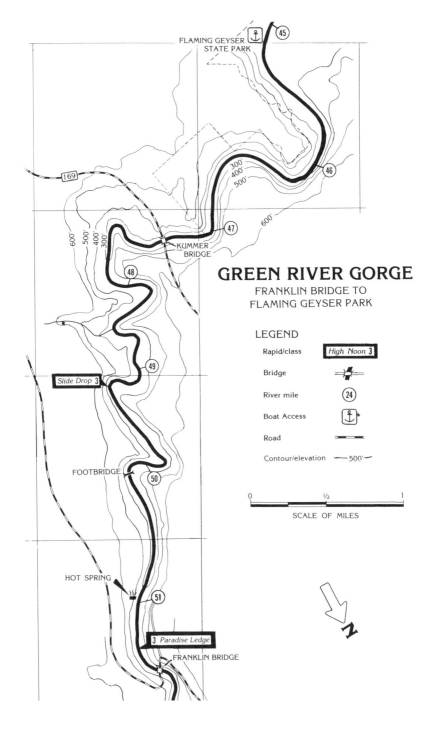

FLAMING GEYSER
STATE PARK

⚓ 45

169

46

300
400
500

600

47

KUMMER
BRIDGE

600
500
400
300

48

49

Slide Drop 3

FOOTBRIDGE

50

HOT SPRING

51

3 Paradise Ledge

FRANKLIN BRIDGE

GREEN RIVER GORGE
FRANKLIN BRIDGE TO
FLAMING GEYSER PARK

LEGEND

Rapid/class	High Noon 3
Bridge	
River mile	24
Boat Access	⚓
Road	
Contour/elevation	500'

0   ½   1

SCALE OF MILES

N

RIVER MILE	RIVER TIME	LEFT BANK	RAPIDS	RIGHT BANK	DESCRIPTION
	4:00				
	55				
	50				
	45				
RM 45	40				
	35	⚓			— Take-out at Flaming Geyser State Park, left
	30				
	25				
	20				
	15		●2		
	10				
	5		●2		
			●2		
	3:00				
	55	⇦	●3		— Highway bridge (Kummer Bridge)
	50		●2 ●3		— Easy class 3
	45		●2 ●2		— Difficult class 2
	40		●2 ●2		— Run right
	35		●2 ●2		— Fish hatchery outlet, left
	30		●3		— **Slide Drop,** scout left on slide area, run left of pillow rock
	25	⇦	●2 ●2		— Scenic cliffs, hanging gardens right
RM 50	20		●2 ●2		— Good surfing waves
					— Footbridge and pipeline
	15		●2 ●2		— Run far right
	10		●3 ●3		— Run center or right
					— Cable crossing
					— Hot spring left, near telephone pole in draw
	5		●3 ●3		— **Paradise Ledge,** great playspot
	2:00		●2		— Put-in, pay at resort to carry boat 150′ (vertical)

17

Skykomish

Logged at - 2,400 cfs Gold Bar gauge
Recommended water level - 2,000 to 5,000 cfs
Best time - July to early August
Rating - Expert
Water level information - NOAA Tape (206) 526-8530
NOAA Information (206) 526-6087
River mile - 50 to 43.5; 6.5 miles
Time - 1 hour, 40 minutes; 3.9 mph
Elevation - 455' to 255'; 31' per mile

Flying through the Airplane Turn in Boulder Drop. *(Rocky Perko photo)*

Powerline to Gold Bar

The Skykomish River is the charter river in Washington State's scenic river program and provides a wide variety of river trips. Most of the rapids are above the town of Gold Bar (named by prospectors in 1869) because of a change in the underlying geology. Below Gold Bar the rocks of the Western Metamorphic Zone are relatively soft sandstones and mudstones which erode easily to create a smooth, constantly sloping riverbed and a broad valley. Above Gold Bar, the rocks of the Eastern Metamorphic Zone are considerably harder and make for more rapids and a narrower river valley.

This section of the Sky is in the Eastern Metamorphic Zone and has the best rapids on the main stem of the river. The most outstanding rapid, Boulder Drop, is class 4 at most of the water levels recommended in this guide but is shown as a class 5 because it reaches that level of difficulty at the upper end of the recommended range. Due to the difficulty of the section, county law requires that all boaters wear both helmets and lifejackets. Wetsuits should also be worn because the water is cold and the chances of a long swim are good. For those who are prepared, the Sky provides one of the most exciting and beautiful whitewater experiences in Washington.

Getting There

The Skykomish River is paralleled by US 2 about 50 miles northeast of Seattle.

Put-ins and Take-outs

From Gold Bar the put-in is reached by turning off US 2 onto Mt. Index Road south of the river, immediately before the US 2 bridge that crosses the river near Index. Drive approximately 0.5 mile on a dirt road and pull off on the left (river side) just beyond some power lines crossing overhead. From here, a steep trail leads down through the woods to a pool in the river, just above a series of power lines. This is one of the few spots along the river that is National Forest land. You should not put in farther upriver because private property must be crossed to do so. As of this writing, the state of Washington is still developing a management plan for the river. I hope the plan, once completed, will call for easements along the river creating an easier put-in. Until easements have been secured, most property along the river is privately owned, and trespassing is not permitted. Parking is available near the put-in but is limited.

The take-out is reached on an unmarked dirt road about 100 yards east of the US 2 bridge just above Gold Bar. A Department of Wildlife conservation license is required to use this access — a dirt parking area next to an eddy just below the bridge.

An alternative put-in or take-out point is just below the railroad bridge at log time 50 minutes. It is a steep 100-yard carry and recommended for light boats only. It is found at a small dirt turnout on the outside of a bend on US 2 about a mile above Zeke's drive-in. There is only room for about four cars, so park all the rest of your vehicles elsewhere and leave only one shuttle car here.

Water Level

The Skykomish is a good run at 2,000 to 5,000 cfs on the Gold Bar gauge. Only those who know the river well should run it at above 5,000 cfs.

Skykomish
Gold Bar Gauge
Recommend 2,000 to 5,000 cfs

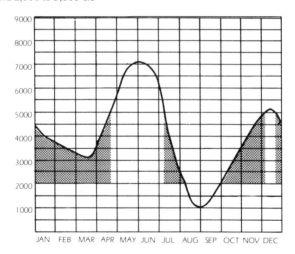

Special Hazards

None, other than **Boulder Drop.**

Scenery

This pool-and-drop river is a very pretty blue-green but uninvitingly cold. A boulder-choked part of the Washington State Scenic Rivers System, the Sky provides breathtaking views of Mt. Index and

Riding out the tail-waves of Boulder Drop

Mt. Persis. Both of these peaks tower some 5,000 feet above a riverbank that is covered by evergreen and deciduous trees. It is one of the cleanest rivers in western Washington, with very few logs to mar its granite boulder bed.

Camping

Forest Service campgrounds can be found at Money Creek, about 11 miles up US 2, or at Troublesome Creek and San Juan, 11 and 13 miles respectively up the North Fork of the Skykomish River.

Rapids

Powerline, the first rapid, can be seen from the put-in. Normally a class 3 drop, at high water levels (above 3,500 cfs to 4,500 cfs), the drop may be considered class 4. You should start your run on the left to avoid a large hole near the top of the rapid and then move to the center. The entire rapid can be scouted from the left side.

At log time 30 minutes, the Skykomish enters a rapid that kayakers have long referred to as **Garbage.** The favored route is to the left with the majority of water.

Anderson Hole is about 30 minutes from the put-in. It is formed by a large rock and hole in the middle of the river where Anderson Creek enters the Skykomish. This hole can flip a kayak or raft. A safe run can be made through a small gap to the left and through an easier and larger passage to the right. The right route is recommended, as Boulder Drop is reached some 150 yards after Anderson Hole and should be scouted on the right bank.

Boulder Drop is recognized from upstream by a large number of house-sized boulders crossing the river as it constricts. Scouting from the right bank will reveal that the rapid consists of at least three distinct drops. Each drop must be carefully negotiated through a narrow passage. All scouting or portaging must be done on the right bank on National Forest land; the left bank is privately owned and no trespassing is allowed. The first drop is run on the right over a number of completely or partially submerged boulders which, at some water levels, can create troublesome holes. Approximately 20 yards below this drop, the boater reaches the second and principal drop. It is known as the Pickets because of four large boulders staggered at regular (more or less) intervals across the river. Two routes are commonly run through this section: the Needle or the Airplane Turn.

BOULDER NOTES

A. Entrance to rapid, small reversal; push through—don't hold back.

B. Submerged rock and breaking wave. Use wave to push boat to left.

C. Bad reversal; go left.

D. The Needle. Reversal at bottom pushes boat hard left.

E. The Dragon's Back. Easy to hang up on after needle; run just to the right but avoid breaking wave downstream on the right.

F. The Airplane Turn route. Run right of double reversals.

G. Alternative route not preferred.

H. House Rock.

I. Combination reversal and breaking waves. Run left portion.

J. Mercy Chute.

Drawing at 4,000 cfs

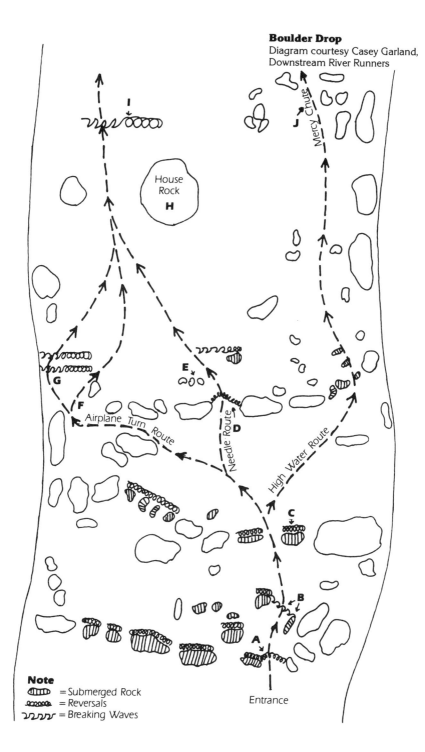

Boulder Drop
Diagram courtesy Casey Garland,
Downstream River Runners

Mercy Chute

House
Rock
H

Airplane Turn Route

Needle Route

High Water Route

Entrance

Note
= Submerged Rock
= Reversals
= Breaking Waves

There are lots of good playspots on the Sky

The Needle is the steep route, directly between the two middle rocks. Most of the water pours through the Needle. However, due to the number of rocks at the bottom of the drop, the Needle cannot ordinarily be run with less than 2,000 cfs. Below the Needle, you are usually pushed to the left against an exposed rock by the force of the water. After pushing by this rock, it is necessary to move even farther

Surfing the blue-green waters of the Sky

left. There is a considerable drop alongside the house-sized rock below, but it is easily negotiated if you are still in control of your craft.

The Airplane Turn is probably the easier route to take if you can make the ferry to reach the turn. After negotiating the first drop, it is necessary to make a strong ferry to the left of the river, going around the left end of the Pickets. This route is not immediately obvious and requires careful study. Once you have managed to get far enough left to avoid the pull of the current toward the Needle, the water will carry you to the left into the turn. Turn 90 degrees and sweep right, back over a small ledge, toward the center of the river. After the Airplane Turn, the run to the left of the house-sized rock is usually not difficult.

If you decide to portage Boulder Drop, it should be done on the north bank of the river. The landowner on the south bank does not want boaters on his property. The portage can be made over the large boulders along the bank or up the slope to the railroad grade, along the grade, and then back down to the river.

After running Boulder Drop, you soon reach **The Ledge, Marble-shoot** and **Lunch Hole.** Lunch Hole should be run on the right, as a huge hole forms on the left on the outside of the bend.

At log time 50 minutes, you reach the Burlington Northern railroad bridge. Kayakers often take out here as most of the whitewater is over. From the bridge on, the river remains exciting, although not of the same class, and more private property dots the shore as the river broadens.

The take-out is easily recognized by the US 2 highway bridge. For the unwary, the last few yards before the take-out can be quite a surprise. The river unexpectedly drops under the bridge, and most of the river runs right, ending the trip with a jolt. The take-out itself is on the left bank next to a large eddy just downstream of the bridge.

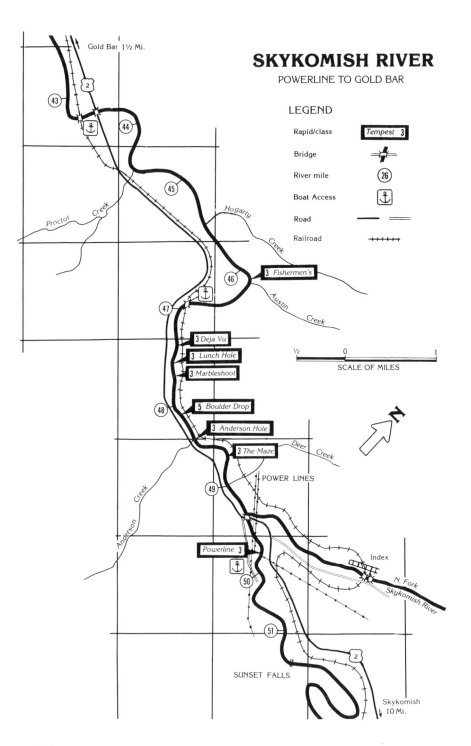

SKYKOMISH RIVER
POWERLINE TO GOLD BAR

LEGEND

Rapid/class	Tempest 3
Bridge	
River mile	26
Boat Access	⚓
Road	
Railroad	+++++

Gold Bar 1½ Mi.

2

43

⚓

44

45

Proctor Creek

Hogarty

Creek

46

⚓

3 Fishermen's

47

Austin Creek

3 Deja Vu

3 Lunch Hole

3 Marbleshoot

5 Boulder Drop

48

3 Anderson Hole

3 The Maze

Deer Creek

POWER LINES

49

Anderson Creek

½   0   1

SCALE OF MILES

N

Powerline 3

⚓

50

Index

N. Fork
Skykomish River

51

2

SUNSET FALLS

Skykomish
10 Mi.

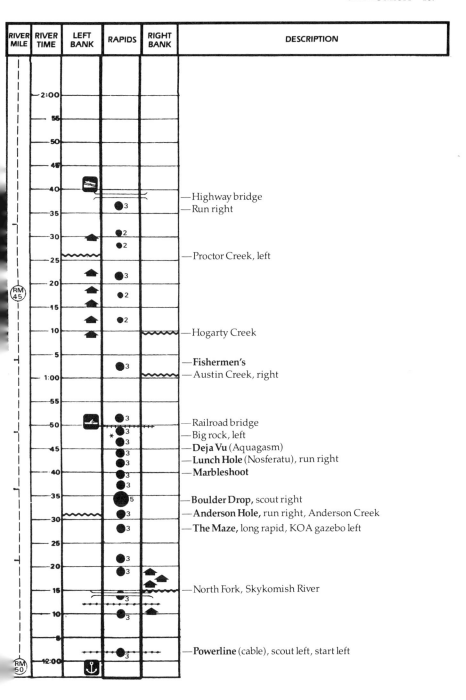

RIVER MILE	RIVER TIME	LEFT BANK	RAPIDS	RIGHT BANK	DESCRIPTION
	2:00				
	55				
	50				
	45				
	40				—Highway bridge
	35		●3		—Run right
	30		●2		
			●2		
	25				—Proctor Creek, left
	20		●3		
	15		●2		
	10		●2		
RM 45					—Hogarty Creek
	5				—**Fishermen's**
	1:00		●3		—Austin Creek, right
	55				
	50		●3		—Railroad bridge
			*●3		—Big rock, left
	45		●3		—**Deja Vu** (Aquagasm)
			●3		—**Lunch Hole** (Nosferatu), run right
	40		●3		—**Marbleshoot**
			●3		
	35		●5		—**Boulder Drop,** scout right
	30		●3		—**Anderson Hole,** run right, Anderson Creek
			●3		—**The Maze,** long rapid, KOA gazebo left
	25				
	20		●3		
			●3		
	15				—North Fork, Skykomish River
			●3		
	10		●3		
					—**Powerline** (cable), scout left, start left
RM 50	12:00		●3		

Appendix

In 1986, the Washington State Legislature passed a law governing commercial river running. While the provisions apply only to commercial trips, all river runners should comply with some of the sections. **Section 3** requires that all watercraft be operated in a careful and prudent manner and that no watercraft interfere with other watercraft or proper navigation of the river. **Section 9** spells out the reporting requirements in the event that a person dies or disappears.

Chapter 91.14—Passenger Watercraft for Hire—Operation

Sec.

91.14.005.   Purpose

The purpose of this chapter is to further the public interest, welfare, and safety by providing for the protection and promotion of safety in the operation of watercraft carrying passengers for hire on the rivers of this state.

Enacted by Laws 1986, ch 217, § 1.

91.14.010.   Definitions.

Unless the context clearly requires otherwise, the definitions in this section apply throughout this chapter.

The Green River Gorge has challenging whitewater amid beautiful scenery

(1) "Watercraft" means every type of watercraft carrying passengers for hire used as a means of transportation on a river, including but not limited to power boats, drift boats, open canoes, inflatable crafts, decked canoes, and kayaks.

(2) "Carrying passengers for hire" means carrying passengers by watercraft for valuable consideration, whether given directly or indirectly or received by the owner, agent, operator, or other persons having an interest in the watercraft. This shall not affect trips where expenses for food, transportation, or incidentals are shared by participants on an even basis. Anyone receiving compensation for skills or money for amortization of equipment and carrying passengers shall be considered to be carrying passengers for hire. Individuals licensed under chapter 77.32 RCW and acting as a fishing guide are exempt from this chapter.

(3) "Operate" means to navigate or otherwise use a watercraft.

(4) "Operator" means any person operating the watercraft or performing the duties of a pilot or guide for one or more watercraft in a group.

(5) "Passenger" means every person on board a watercraft who is not an operator.

(6) "Rivers of the state" means those rivers and streams, or parts thereof, within the boundaries of this state.

Enacted by Laws 1986, ch. 217, § 2.

91.14.020. Operation of watercraft

(1) No person may operate any watercraft in a manner that interferes with other watercraft or with the free and proper navigation of the rivers of this state.

(2) Every operator of a watercraft shall at all times operate the watercraft in a careful and prudent manner and at such a speed as to not endanger the life, limb, or property of any person.

(3) No watercraft may be loaded with passengers or cargo beyond its safe carrying capacity taking into consideration the type and construction of the watercraft and other existing operating conditions. In the case of inflatable crafts, safe carrying capacity in whitewater shall be considered as less than the United States Coast Guard capacity rating for each watercraft. This subsection shall not apply in cases of an unexpected emergency on the river.

Enacted by Laws 1986, ch. 217, § 3.

91.14.030. Watercraft rights of way

(1) Except as provided in subsection (2) of this section, watercraft proceeding downstream have the right of way over watercraft proceeding upstream.

(2) In all cases, watercraft not under power have the right of way over motorized craft underway.

Enacted by Laws 1986, ch. 217, § 4.

91.14.040. Operators — First aid card required — Exception

(1) No person may operate on the rivers of this state a watercraft carrying

passengers for hire unless the person has been issued a valid Red Cross standard first aid card or at least its equivalent.

(2) This section does not apply to a person operating a vessel on the navigable waters of the United States in this state and who is licensed by the United States Coast Guard for the type of vessel being operated.

Enacted by Laws 1986, ch. 217, § 5.

91.14.050. Safety equipment

While carrying passengers for hire on whitewater river sections in this state, the operator and owner shall:

(1) If using inflatable watercraft, use only watercraft with three or more separate air chambers;

(2) Ensure that all passenger and operators are wearing a securely fastened United States Coast Guard approved type III or type V life jacket in good condition;

(3) Ensure that each watercraft has accessible a spare type III or type V life jacket in good repair;

(4) Ensure that each watercraft has on it a bagged throwable line with a floating line and bag;

(5) Ensure that each watercraft has accessible an adequate first-aid kit;

(6) Ensure that each watercraft has a spare propelling device;

(7) Ensure that a repair kit and air pump are accessible to inflatable watercraft; and

(8) Ensure that equipment to prevent and treat hypothermia is accessible to all watercraft on a trip.

Enacted by Laws 1986, ch. 217, § 6.

91.14.060. Whitewater river sections — Use of alcohol prohibited — Watercraft to be accompanied by other watercraft

(1) Watercraft operators and passengers on any trip carrying passengers for hire shall not allow the use of alcohol during the course of a trip on a whitewater river section in this state.

(2) Any watercraft carrying passengers for hire on any whitewater river section in this state must be accompanied by at least one other watercraft under the supervision of the same operator or owner or being operated by a person registered under RCW 91.14.090 or an operator under the direction or control of a person registered under RCW 91.14.090.

Enacted by Laws 1986, ch. 217, § 7.

91.14.070. Whitewater river sections — Designation

Whitewater river sections include but are not limited to:

(1) Green river above Flaming Geyser state park;

(2) Klickitat river above the confluence with Summit creek;

(3) Methow river below the town of Carlton;

(4) Sauk river above the town of Darrington;

(5) Skagit river above Bacon creek;

(6) Suiattle river;

(7) Tieton river below Rimrock dam;

(8) Skykomish river below Sunset Falls and above the Highway 2 bridge one mile east of the town of Gold Bar;

(9) Wenatchee river above the Wenatchee county park at the town of Monitor;

(10) White Salmon river; and

(11) Any other section of river designated a "whitewater river section" by the interagency committee for outdoor recreation. Such river sections shall be class two or greater difficulty under the international scale of whitewater difficulty.

Enacted by Laws 1986, ch. 217, § 8.

91.14.080.   Death or disappearance from watercraft — Notification of authorities

(1) When, as a result of an occurrence that involves a watercraft or its equipment, a person dies or disappears from a watercraft, the operator shall notify the nearest sheriff's department, state patrol office, coast guard station, or other law enforcement agency of:

(a) The date, time, and exact location of the occurrence;

(b) The name of each person who died or disappeared;

(c) A description of the watercraft; and

(d) The names and addresses of the owner and operator.

(2) When the operator of a boat cannot give the notice required by subsection (1) of this section, each person on board that boat shall either give the notice or determine that the notice has been given.

Enacted by Laws 1986, ch. 217, § 9.

91.14.090.   Registration of persons carrying passengers for hire on whitewater river sections — List of registered persons — Notice of registrants' insurance termination — State immune from civil actions arising from registration

(1) Any person carrying passengers for hire on whitewater river sections in this state may register with the department of licensing. Each registration application shall be submitted annually on a form provided by the department of licensing and shall include the following information:

(a) The name, residence address, and residence telephone number, and the business name, address, and telephone number of the registrant;

(b) Proof that the registrant has liability insurance for a minimum of three hundred thousand dollars per claim for occurrences by the registrant and the registrant's employees that result in bodily injury or property damage; and

(c) Certification that the registrant will maintain the insurance for a period of not less than one year from the date of registration.

(2) The department of licensing shall charge a fee for each application, to be set in accordance with RCW 43.24.086.

(3) Any person advertising or representing themselves as having registered under this section who is not currently registered is guilty of a gross misdemeanor.

(4) The department of licensing shall submit annually a list of registered persons and companies to the department of trade and economic development, tourism promotion division.

(5) If an insurance company cancels or refuses to renew insurance for a registrant during the period of registration, the insurance company shall notify the department of licensing in writing of the termination of coverage and its effective date not less than thirty days before the effective date of termination.

(a) Upon receipt of an insurance company termination notice, the department of licensing shall send written notice to the registrant that on the effective date of termination the department of licensing will suspend the registration unless proof of insurance as required by this section is filed with the department of licensing before the effective date of the termination.

(b) If an insurance company fails to give notice of coverage termination, this failure shall not have the effect of continuing the coverage.

(c) The department of licensing may suspend or revoke registration under this section if the registrant fails to maintain in full force and effect the insurance required by this section.

(6) The state of Washington shall be immune from any civil action arising from a registration under this section.

Enacted by Laws 1986, ch. 217, § 11.

91.14.100. Enforcement — Chapter to supplement federal law

(1) Every peace officer of this state and its political subdivisions has the authority to enforce this chapter. Wildlife agents of the department of game and fisheries patrol officers of the department of fisheries, through their directors, the state patrol, through its chief, county sheriffs, and other local law enforcement bodies, shall assist in the enforcement. In the exercise of this responsibility, all such officers may stop any watercraft and direct it to a suitable pier or anchorage for boarding.

(2) A person, while operating a watercraft on any waters of this state, shall not knowingly flee or attempt to elude a law enforcement officer after having received a signal from the law enforcement officer to bring the boat to a stop.

(3) This chapter shall be construed to supplement federal laws and regulations. To the extent this chapter is inconsistent with federal laws and regulations, the federal laws and regulations shall control.

Enacted by Laws 1986, ch. 217, § 10.

91.14.110. Civil penalty

A person violating this chapter shall be subject to a civil penalty of up to one hundred fifty dollars per violation.

Enacted by Laws 1986, ch. 217, § 12.

INDEX

Index

Airplane Turn, 162,163,165
Alligator Drop, 142
Anderson Hole, 162
Annapurna, 79
Another Roadside Attraction, 122

Bedal Campground, 52-53
Black Canyon Rapids, 125
Boulder Bend, 74,76-77
Boulder Creek Rapids, 133
Boulder Drop, 160,162-63,165
BZ Corner, 98,106,108

Camp Four, 130-31
Carlton, 120,122,125
Concrete Bridge, 47,115-16
Copper Creek, 58-59,61
Corkscrew Falls, 110,111
Cottonwood rapid, 41
Cubic Feet per Second, 16

100,120,132
Darrington, 53,65,138,140
Demon Seed. *See* Jaws
Douglas Fir Campground, 90,91,93
Drunkard's Drop, 74,78

Eskimo Roll, 27

Falls Creek Campground, 133
Falls Creek Rapids, 131
Federal Wild & Scenic Rivers Act,
29-31,47,53,58,65,84,91,97,
108,115,121,132,138
Five Mile Bridge, 130
Flaming Geyser Park, 147,149

Garbage, 162
Gold Bar, 159-60
Goodell Creek, 58,61
Granny's Rapid, 79
Grasshopper, 110,111

Horseshoe Bend, 39,40
House Rocks Drop, 117
Hurricane, 67
Husum Falls, 110-11

Jaws, 142-43

K-2, 79

La Wis Wis, 32-35
Leavenworth, 72,74,76
Ledge Drop 1, 150-51
Leidl Bridge, 97-99
Lunch Hole, 165

Maple Falls, 91
Marbleshoot, 165
Maytag Drop, 111
Mercury, 151-53
Meteorite, 125
Monitor, 72,74

National Oceanic and Atmospheric
Administration, 17
Needle, The, 162,163,164
NOAA. *See* National Oceanic &
Atmospheric Administration
Northwest Power Planning
Council, 10

The author taping notes on a whitewater trip.

Doug North began running Washington rivers seven years ago as a whitewater canoeist. He was surprised to find out that little information on Washington's whitewater rivers was available in print; particularly lacking was information on good water levels for each trip. So he began compiling information that resulted in his guidebooks — first, *Washington Whitewater 1,* then *Washington Whitewater 2,* and now this revised second edition of the first book.

North is a Washington native and practices law in Seattle. A long-time outdoor enthusiast, he also hikes, climbs and skis cross-country. In addition to boating Washington rivers, he has run nearly a dozen rivers in Colorado, Oregon, Idaho and British Columbia. A founder of Northwest Rivers Council (formerly Friends of Whitewater), he has been very active in protecting the rivers of the Northwest from development that would interfere with their free-flowing qualities and the recreation, fish and wildlife dependent on them.